FRIENDS AND ENEMIES

A Collection of Short Stories

Also available from Collins

Angel Face   Narinder Dhami
Street Child   Berlie Doherty
The Games Board Map   Stephen Elboz
Journey Through Llandor   Louise Lawrence
The Exiles   Hilary McKay
The Shouting Wind   Linda Newbery
Blitz   Robert Westall
A Ruby, A Rug and a Prince Called Doug   Kaye Umansky

FRIENDS AND ENEMIES

edited by Bryan Newton

Collins

An *Imprint* of HarperCollins*Publishers*

First published in Great Britain by
HarperCollins Educational in 1983
First published by Collins in 1995
1 3 5 7 9 8 6 4 2

Collins is an imprint of HarperCollins*Publishers* Ltd.,
77-85 Fulham Palace Road,
Hammersmith, London W6 8JB

ISBN 0 00 675020 6

Printed and bound in Great Britain
by HarperCollins Manufacturing Ltd, Glasgow

CONTENTS

How Anthony Made a Friend *by Jan Mark* 1

Lenny's Red-Letter Day *by Bernard Ashley* 26

The Great Leapfrog Contest *by William Saroyan* 40

The Mile *by George Layton* 52

Duffings *by E. W. Hildick* 70

Cleo the Vigilant *by Tim Kennemore* 81

The Hitch-Hiker *by Roald Dahl* 115

After You, My Dear Alphonse *by Shirley Jackson* 138

Thingy *by Chris Powling* 145

Black Eyes *by Philippa Pearce* 160

KBW *by Farrukh Dhondy* 177

Mart was my Best Friend *by Michael Rosen* 197

HOW ANTHONY MADE A FRIEND

JAN MARK

"We're lucky to get on so well with the people next door," said Mr and Mrs Clayton. "Especially after the last lot."

The last lot had pushed their piano against the party wall and played a tune called 'Friends and Neighbours' at one o'clock in the morning.

"Do you think they're trying to tell us something?" said Mr Clayton, on the seventh or eighth occasion. Mrs Clayton screamed quietly.

"Playing a tune called 'Friends and Neighbours' doesn't qualify them as either, in my opinion," said Mr Clayton, but quite soon afterwards the owners of the piano moved out taking their instrument with them, and the Faulkeners moved in.

Mrs Clayton, watching from the landing window, observed that Mr Faulkener was carrying a double-bass, and hurried down to invite Mrs Faulkener in for a cup of tea. Over the cup of tea she casually mentioned the last occupants and the piano. Mrs Faulkener was quick on the uptake.

"Oh, don't worry about us. We go to bed early," she said.

"They seem a very pleasant couple," said Mrs Clayton, at tea-time. "And they have a little girl, about Anthony's age. She'll be company for Anthony, perhaps."

"Perhaps," said Mr Clayton.

"Her name's Jenny," said Mrs Clayton. "She's staying with her aunt at the moment, but she'll be here on Saturday. Perhaps Anthony could invite her round for tea."

"Perhaps," said Mr Clayton, and made himself busy with the evening paper.

"Would you like that, Anthony?" said Mrs Clayton.

"No," said Anthony. He sat at the end of the table, tearing holes in a slice of bread and butter. Anyone who did not know that he lived there might have been forgiven for thinking that he had drifted in through the keyhole in a cloud of black smoke. He was thin and dark with little eyes like cold cinders. His hair curled up at the front in horns. At school he prowled round the playground by himself, muttering; to himself. When he came home his mother gave him his tea and sent him out to play with his friends in the street, under the impression that he had some friends to play with. He did not. His favourite person was Anthony Clayton, and he had no time for anyone else. He was nine. He looked thirty, but stunted.

Jenny Faulkener arrived on Saturday, as threatened. She was remarkably like her father's double-bass from the neck down, and her hair was plaited into long gingery pigtails.

"Go and ask her to tea," said Mrs Clayton, when Anthony showed signs of disappearing into the cupboard under the stairs.

"I'm playing chess," said Anthony, oozing out again.

"You can't play chess by yourself," said his mother.

9

"I can," said Anthony. "And I'm cheating."

"Don't be silly," said his mother. "Go at once and ask Jenny to tea. They're expecting you."

Anthony went out of his front gate, turned sharp left and in at the Faulkeners' gate. Jenny opened the door before he had taken his finger off the bell-push. They certainly were expecting him.

"I've got to ask you to tea," said Anthony.

"That's right," said Jenny Faulkener. "I'm all ready." She stepped out of the house and closed the door behind her.

"You're not coming now, are you?" said Anthony.

"Why not? It's four o'clock."

"Aren't you going to wash or anything?"

"You're very rude, aren't you?" said Jenny, as they negotiated the gates. "My mother said you were a funny little thing."

"My mother," said Anthony, "*didn't* say you were a fat lump; but you are."

"I shall go home if you talk like that," said Jenny.

"I don't mind," said Anthony, and opened the gate again, so that she could, but Jenny didn't move.

"It's no good trying to get rid of me," she

said, pityingly. "Mummy said that you're only peculiar because you're lonely. We're going to be friends."

"We'll hell as like," said Anthony, but quietly, becuase his mother was opening the door.

"You must be Jenny," she said. "Come in, dear. We're so pleased you've come to live next door to us. Anthony, take Jenny upstairs to play until tea's ready."

"I told you it was too early," said Anthony, as they went up.

Anthony's bedroom was painted pale blue. There was a frilly lampshade hanging from the ceiling and little Donald Ducks on the white window curtains. By the bed lay a fluffy rug with a pussycat worked on it.

"Oh, what a lovely room," cried Jenny, skipping in the sunshine, but then Anthony came in behind her and immediately shadows began to gather in the corners.

"What's that hanging on the bedpost?" said Jenny.

"My noose," said Anthony.

"Are these your books?"

"They're my mother's books," said Anthony. "She buys them for me. These are mine." He turned his back on the row of new and obviously unopened books and pulled out a drawer at the bottom of the wardrobe. Jenny saw squat volumes in crumbling black leather. A smell of old libraries hung about them, of librarians dead and gone.

"What are they about?"

"I don't know," said Anthony. "They're all in Latin. I get them off a stall in the market."

"Why buy them if you can't understand what they say?"

"I like the look of them," said Anthony.

Jenny looked at him. She could believe it.

"Does your mother always call you Anthony?"

"Yes."

"Doesn't anyone ever call you Tony?"

"No," said Anthony.

"I shall."

"No you won't."

"You can't stop me."

"I shan't take any notice, so you can save your breath," said Anthony, savagely.

"My name's Jennifer, but everyone calls me Jenny, except Auntie May. Auntie calls me Angel-face. I'm not going to call you Anthony."

"You're not going to call me Angel-face either," said Anthony, twirling his noose.

"I'll call you An*th*ony," said Jenny. "That's how it's spelt."

Anthony looked daunted for once. "You can't do that. It sounds silly."

"Yes, it does," Jenny agreed. "But you shouldn't have an 'h' in it if you don't want people to say it."

Mrs Clayton poked a winsome smile round the door.

"Tea-time, children."

"Ooh, lovely," said Jenny, with a smile every bit as winsome. "Come along, An*th*ony." She grabbed him by the wrist and yanked him out of the bedroom. She was horribly strong.

"She seems a very sweet child," said Mrs Clayton, watching Jenny drag Anthony down the street next day. "I think she'll bring him out of himself."

"Is that a good thing?" said Mr Clayton. "Remember Pandora's box."

Anthony, had he been present, would have agreed with his father. He had barely reached the front gate that morning, when the Faulkeners' window went up with a crash and Jenny leaned out, carolling, "An*th*oneeee! Wait for meeee!"

He had run, but she ran faster.

"Let's play mothers and fathers," said Jenny.

"Let's play hangman," said Anthony. "I'll be the hangman." He was beginning to realize that having friends might be a good thing after all. There was safety in numbers.

"Are you adopted?" said Jenny.

"What do you mean?"

"Mummy said you might be, because you're so dark and your parents are so fair."

"I'm a throwback," Anthony growled. Jenny did not know what he meant, but if such things existed Anthony was definitely one. Someone should throw him back immediately.

"I think you're a changeling," she confided. "I think the fairies stole the real Clayton baby and left you in its place."

"I think you're a fat loony," said Anthony.

Fortunately Jenny went to a different school, but as soon as she arrived home, five minutes after he did, she appeared at the door, or scrambled over the back fence.

"Anthony!"

"Glutton for punishment," said Mr Clayton.

"I think Anthony likes her really, but he's too shy to show it," said Mrs Clayton.

"Shy?" said her husband. "If he's shy, I'm King Kong. Why don't you face facts?"

Winter drew near, Anthony's favourite season, when trees shivered naked in the fog and the wind howled across the roofing slates. This year was better still, for on murky evenings Mr Faulkener's bull fiddle could be heard lowing like a damned soul in the distance. But so could his daughter.

"Anthony!"

"Now what?"

"Are you going to make a guy?"

"What for?"

"I'd have thought you'd enjoy burning it," said Jenny. "Are you having fireworks?"

"I don't like fireworks," said Anthony, forbearing to add that his mother did not like them either.

"Oh well, you can watch ours. We have a firework party every year and invite all our friends. You can come -"

"I don't *like* fireworks."

"You're my friend. We'll make the guy together."

Mrs Clayton did not really approve of making guys, but she did so like to see Jenny and Anthony side by side, the golden head and the dark one. She rarely troubled to

15

overhear what the dark head had to say to the golden head, which was possibly just as well.

"I bet you've got nits in your pigtails, Codface," said Anthony.

A pyre began to rise in the Faulkeners' garden; tier upon tier of crushed tea-chests, brushwood, off-cuts and old chair-legs. Anthony provided the chair-legs.

"Wherever did you get so many old chair-legs, dear?" said Mrs Faulkener.

"Off old chairs," said Anthony, with a scowl that made Mrs Faulkener want to scurry indoors to see how her furniture was getting along.

Mrs Faulkener and Mrs Clayton each contributed a pile of cast-off clothes to make the guy. Jenny assembled it and Anthony watched. It grew. It swelled. It developed into an elegant creature with a wasp waist and a stunning bosom full of old stockings. Jenny made its head out of a pillow case and painted a face on it with black, long-lashed eyes, rosy cheeks and a cupid's-bow mouth. It sat in a chair and simpered, while Jenny stitched a pink felt hat on its head, trimmed with pigeon feathers.

"It's a lady guy," said Jenny. "I'm going to call it Guyella."

"It looks like you," said Anthony.

"Have you seen the children's guy?" said Mrs Faulkener to Mrs Clayton. Anthony realised that he was being held jointly responsible for the monstrous dolly, and saw his reputation in ruins. There were still some old clothes left over and he set about constructing a rival. Jenny, reasonably enough, had taken the best garments for the first guy, but there remained a bolster case, a pair of black woollen stockings and a sweater or two. Anthony borrowed a needle from his mother and went to work. Next morning Mrs Clayton nearly found an early grave when she discovered Anthony's guy lying across the end of his bed in the cold November light.

Anthony's guy was nine feet long. It had four arms and a pointed head. Its chin was gathered into its neck so that it looked as if it were being strangled, and Anthony had sewn its legs on back to front so that its black woolly toes pointed perversely in the opposite direction from its face.

Anthony came down to breakfast with the guy slung over his shoulder like a fireman rescuing a victim, although it was difficult to imagine Anthony rescuing anyone. After the table was cleared Anthony conducted his guy to the front gate, dragging it by one leg, for maximum effect. In the adjoining gateway Jenny had set up Guyella in an old push-chair, and she was explaining to a neighbour that she and An*th*ony had made it together.

"I hope you are not asking for pennies," said the neighbour. "I always think that that is a kind of begging."

"Oh no," said Jenny, "but it's such a lovely guy, we wanted everyone to see it."

"It's too pretty to burn," said the neighbour, and then let out a dismayed squeak, for looking over Jenny's head she had seen Anthony emerging followed, inch by inch, by his guy.

"Ooh, An*th*ony's made one, too," cried Jenny. Wordlessly, Anthony hoisted his creature to its feet and draped its spineless carcass over the gatepost so that it leered down at Guyella with a speculative eye; one speculative eye.

"Good God," said the neighbour, faintly.

"This is Flabber," said Anthony, deftly arranging the four arms so that the guy had every appearance of swarming up the gatepost and doing something unspeakable on the other side.

"Oh, An*th*ony," said Jenny. "It's horrid."

"I should move Guyella, if I was you," said
Anthony, "before it gets over."

Anthony, who had never been one for teddy-bears and gollywogs, became decidedly attached to Flabber. It slept coiled like a boa constrictor, on the end of his bed, and accompanied him to meals, where it sat slumped on its own chair at the corner of the table.

"Does that revolting thing have to eat with us?" demanded Anthony's father, flicking one of Flabber's four hands away from the cake-plate.

"Sssh, dear. Anthony's so fond of it," said Mrs Clayton.

"That figures," said Mr Clayton.

Mrs Faulkener did not care for Flabber either. "Perhaps you'd like to leave it in the garden?" she suggested, when Anthony came round to play, with his invertebrate chum lagging his narrow neck.

"It will get cold, poor sweet," said Anthony, in a voice that was suspiciously similar to Jenny's. He went upstairs and Flabber slithered behind, its pointed head knocking softly on each step.

All the same, it was Guyella who attracted the praise and attention. People stopped to admire Guyella, and if they admired Flabber, they preferred not to mention it. Also, Jenny with her golden plaits was more approachable than swarthy and surly Anthony.

"That thing gives me the creeps," Mr Faulkener complained, after a high wind dislodged Flabber and he found it lying across his gateway.

"Never mind," said Mrs Faulkener. "They'll be burning it on Friday."

"But not little Anthony, alas," said Mr Faulkener, and Mrs Faulkener was deeply shocked, because her husband was a kindly man and loved children.

Anthony, as it happened, was at that moment leaning over the bannisters.

Next morning, Flabber and Guyella were put out to take the air as usual, but quite early on Jenny was sent to the corner shop to buy biscuits for elevenses. When she returned, Guyella had gone.

Jenny wept. "Why didn't you keep an eye on them?" she demanded, when Anthony came out to see what the keening was about.

"I was busy," Anthony said. What a good thing Flabber wasn't stolen as well." For Flabber was still clinging like a squid to the gatepost. It looked smug, almost sleek, on account of its fortunate escape. One might have imagined that it had put on weight. It had hips, where no hips had been before.

Inquiries were made up and down the street, but no one had been abducting Guyella. "I expect it was those boys from down the Lane," was the best help anyone could give.

"Well, darling, you've still got Anthony's er - guy," said Mrs Faulkener.

"I wish they'd pinched that instead," said Jenny.

"Don't be selfish," said her mother, who was thinking the same thing. "And don't say 'pinched'. It sounds so common."

November the Fifth arrived, but Guyella did not come home. Jenny was consoled with boxes of fireworks, and went round to remind Anthony that the party started at seven.

"Shall I take Flabber now, Anthony? So that Daddy can put him on the bonfire?"

"No," said Anthony. "He's coming with me."

"But he ought to be up there ready when the party starts."

"Then I'll come early," said Anthony.

Mr and Mrs Clayton and Anthony and Flabber arrive early, as promised, but so did all the other guests, who were mostly friends and neighbours from the Faulkeners' old home, so there was a fair-sized crowd assembled with torches when the great row took place. Some of the friends and neighbours looked taken aback when Flabber loomed out of the darkness, suspended from Mrs Clayton's clothes prop. Mr Faulkener put on his gardening gloves and squared up to Flabber with tremendous good humour.

"Right my lad. Up you go."

Anthony jerked the clothes prop. Flabber curtsied and receded into the night.

"We've only come to watch," said Anthony.

"I understood we were going to burn it," said Mr Faulkener, his good humour slipping a little.

"Don't be silly, dear," said Mrs Clayton.

"No! No! I don't want it burned," Anthony yelled, swinging the prop wildly so that Flabber sashayed in and out of the torch light.

"Well, we're going to burn it, Anthony Clayton, so there!" Jenny shouted, and darting forward she seized Flabber by its retrograde feet. Simultaneously, Anthony dropped the clothes prop and flung his arms round Flabber's chest. They both dug their heels in and tugged. The grown-ups tutted and shuffled, and one voice in the dark muttered, "Oh, that *awful* child." Mrs Clayton hoped it meant Jenny. Everyone else assumed it meant Anthony.

Jenny and Anthony meanwhile, teeth clenched, surged back and forth with Flabber horribly stretched out taut between them. Suddenly there was a loud ripping sound and certain vital threads gave way. Jenny sat down hard with Flabber's legs in her lap, while Anthony rolled over backwards, clutching the major remains of Flabber. From Flabber's martyred body slid Guyella, head first and still smirking. There was a nasty silence until Mrs Clayton cried, "Oh, Anthony! That was very naughty of you to steal poor Jenny's guy."

"You sewed her up in your horrible *thing*!" Jenny wailed.

"I think you should do something about that child," said Mrs Faulkener, but Anthony still lay on the ground with Flabber on top of him. From under the tangled heap came a strange sound that no one had ever heard before. Anthony was laughing.

"Get up at once!" roared his father, but it was all Anthony could do to sit. Still giggling, he pointed a shaking finger at Flabber's other end and shrieked, "*It's having a baby!*"

Anthony was not allowed to stay for the

firework party. With Flabber's short corpse tucked under his arm, he was sent home in disgrace, and told to go straight to bed, which he did. For the first time in his life he fell asleep with a smile on his face.

LENNY'S
RED-LETTER DAY

BY BERNARD ASHLEY

Lenny Fraser is a boy in my class. Well, he's a boy in my class when he comes. But to tell the truth, he doesn't come very often. He stays away from school for a week at a time, and I'll tell you where he is. He's at the shops, stealing things sometimes, but mainly just opening the doors for people. He does it to keep himself warm. I've seen him in our shop. When he opens the door for someone, he stands around inside till he gets sent out. Of course, it's quite warm enough in school, but he hates coming. He's always got long, tangled hair, not very clean, and his clothes are too big or too small, and they call him 'Flea-bag'. He sits at a desk without a partner, and no one wants to hold his hand in games. All right, they're not to blame; but he isn't either. His mother never gets up in the morning, and his house is dirty. It's a house that everybody runs past very quickly.

But Lenny makes me laugh a lot. In the playground he's always saying funny things out of the corner of his mouth. He doesn't smile when he does it. He says these funny things as if he's complaining. For example, when Mr Cox the deputy head came to school in his new car, Lenny came too, that day; but he didn't join in all the admiration. He looked at the little car and said to me, "Anyone missing a skateboard?"

He misses all the really good things, though - the School Journeys and the outing. And it was a big shame about his birthday.

It happens like this with birthdays in our class. Miss Blake lets everyone bring their cards and perhaps a small present to show the others. Then everyone sings "Happy Birthday" and we give them bumps in the playground. If people can't bring a present, they tell everyone what they've got instead. I happen to know some people make up things that they've got just to be up with the others, but Miss Blake says it's good to share our Red-Letter Days.

I didn't know about these Red-Letter Days before. I thought they were something special in the post, like my dad handles in his Post Office in the shop. But Miss Blake told us they are red painted words in the prayer book, meaning special days.

Well, what I'm telling you is that Lenny came to school on his birthday this year. Of course, he didn't tell us it was his birthday, and, as it all worked out, it would have been better if Miss Blake hadn't noticed it in the register. But, "How nice!" she said. "Lenny's here on his birthday, and we can share it with him."

It wasn't very nice for Lenny. He didn't have any cards to show the class, and he couldn't think of a birthday present to tell us about. He couldn't even think of anything funny to say out of the corner of his mouth. He just had to stand there looking foolish until Miss Blake started the singing of "Happy Birthday" - and then half the people didn't bother to sing it. I felt very sorry for him, I tell you. But that wasn't the worst. The worst happened in the playground. I went to take his head end for bumps, and no one would come and take his feet. They all walked away. I had to finish up just patting him on the head with my hands, and before I knew what was coming out I was telling him, "You can come home to tea with me, for your birthday." And he said, yes, he would come.

My father works very hard in the Post Office, in a corner of our shop; and my mother stands at the door all day, where people pay for their groceries. When I get home from school, I carry cardboard boxes out to the yard and jump on them, or my big sister Nalini shows me which shelves to fill and I fill them with jam or chapatis - or birthday cards. On this day, though, I thought I'd use my key and go in through the side door and take Lenny straight upstairs - then hurry down again and tell my mum and dad that I'd got a friend in for an hour. I thought, I can get a birthday card and some cake and ice-cream from the shop, and Lenny can go home before they come upstairs. I wanted him to do that before my dad saw who it was, because he knows Lenny from his hanging around the shops.

Lenny said some funny things on the way home from school, but you know, I couldn't relax and enjoy them properly. I felt ashamed because I was wishing all the time that I hadn't asked him to come home with me. The bottoms of his trousers dragged along the ground, he had no buttons on his shirt so the sleeves flapped, and his hair must have made it hard for him to see where he was going.

I was in luck because the shop was very busy. My dad had a queue of people to pay out, and my mum had a crowd at the till. I left Lenny in the living-room and I went down to get what I wanted from the shop. I found him a birthday card with a badge in it. When I came back, he was sitting in a chair and the television was switched on. He's a good one at helping himself, I thought. We watched some cartoons and then we played Monopoly, which Lenny had seen on the shelf. We had some crisps and cakes and lemonade while we were playing but I had only one eye on my Monopoly moves - the other eye was on the clock all the time. I was getting very impatient for the game to finish, because it looked as if Lenny would still be there when they came up from the shop. I did some really bad moves so that I could lose quickly, but it's very difficult to hurry up Monopoly, as you may know.

In the end I did such stupid things - like buying too many houses and selling Park Lane and Mayfair - that he won the game. He must have noticed what I was doing, but he didn't say anything to me. Hurriedly, I gave him his birthday card. He pretended not to take very much notice of it, but he put it in his shirt, and kept feeling it to make sure it was still there. At least, that's what I thought he was making sure about, there inside his shirt.

It was just the right time to say goodbye, and I'm just thinking he can go without anyone seeing him, when my sister came in. She had run up from the shop for something or other, and she put her head inside the room. At some other time, I would have laughed out loud at her stupid face. When she saw Lenny, she looked as if she'd opened the door and seen something really unpleasant. I could gladly have given her a good kick. She shut the door a lot quicker than she opened it, and I felt really bad about it.

"Nice to meet you," Lenny joked, but his face said he wanted to go too, and I wasn't going to be the one to stop him.

I let him out, and I heaved a big sigh. I felt good about being kind to him, the way you do when you've done a sponsored swim, and I'd done it without my mum and dad frowning at me about who I brought home. Only Nalini had seen him, and everyone knows she can make things seem worse than they are. I washed the glasses, and I can remember singing while I stood at the sink. I was feeling very pleased with myself.

My good feeling lasted about fifteen minutes; just long enough to be wearing off slightly. Then Nalini came in again and destroyed it altogether.

"Prakash, have you seen that envelope that was on the television top?" she asked. "I put it on here when I came in from school."

"No," I said. It was very soon to be getting worried, but things inside me were turning over like clothes in a washing-machine. I knew already where all this was going to end up. "What was in it?" My voice sounded to me as if it was coming from a great distance.

She was looking everywhere in the room, but she kept coming back to the television top as if the envelope would mysteriously appear there. She stood there now, staring at me. "*What was in it?* What was in it was only a

Postal Order for five pounds! Money for my school trip!"

"It's a white piece of paper in a brown envelope. It says 'Postal Order' on it, in red."

My washing-machine inside nearly went into a fast spin when I heard that. It was certainly Lenny's Red-Letter Day! But how could he be so ungrateful, I thought, when I was the only one to be kind to him? I clenched my fist while I pretended to look around. I wanted to punch him hard on the nose.

Then Nalini said what was in both our minds. "It's that dirty kid who's got it. I'm going down to tell Dad. I don't know what makes you so stupid."

Right at that moment I didn't know what made me so stupid, either, as to leave him up there on his own. I should have known. Didn't Miss Blake once say something about leopards never changing their spots?

When the shop closed, there was an awful business in the room. My dad was shouting-angry at me, and my mum couldn't think of anything good to say.

"You know where this boy lives," my dad said. "Tell me now, while I telephone the police. There's only one way of dealing with this sort of thing. If I go up there, I shall only get a mouthful of abuse. As if it isn't bad enough for you to see me losing things out of the shop, you have to bring untrustworthy people upstairs!"

My mum saw how unhappy I was, and she tried to make things better. "Can't you cancel the Postal Order?" she asked him.

"Of course not. Even if he hasn't had the time to cash it somewhere else by now, how long do you think the Post Office would let me be Sub-Postmaster if I did that sort of thing?"

I was feeling very bad for all of us, but the thought of the police calling at Lenny's house was making me feel worse.

"I'll get it back," I said. "I'll go to his house. It's only along the road from the school. And if I don't get it back, I can get the exact number of where he lives. *Then* you can telephone the police." I had never spoken to my dad like that before, but I was feeling all shaky inside, and all the world seemed a different place to me that evening. I didn't give anybody a chance to argue with me. I ran straight out of the room and down to the street.

My secret hopes of seeing Lenny before I

got to his house didn't come to anything. All too quickly I was there, pushing back his broken gate and walking up the cracked path to his front door. There wasn't a door knocker. I flapped the letter-box, and I started to think my dad was right. The police would have been better doing this than me.

I had never seen his mother before, only heard about her from other kids who lived near. When she opened the door, I could see she was a small lady with a tight mouth and eyes that said, "Who are you" and "Go away from here!" at the same time.

She opened the door only a little bit, ready to slam it on me. I had to be quick.

"Is Lenny in, please?" I asked her.

She said, "What's it to you?"

"He's a friend of mine," I told her. "Can I see him, please?"

She made a face as if she had something nasty in her mouth. "LENNY!" she shouted. "COME HERE!"

Lenny came slinking down the passage, like one of those scared animals in a circus. He kept his eyes on her hands, once he'd seen who it was at the door. There weren't any funny remarks coming from him.

She jerked her head at me. "How many

times have I told you not to bring kids to the house?" she shouted at him. She made it sound as if she was accusing him of a bad crime.

Lenny had nothing to say. She was hanging over him like a vulture about to fix its talons into a rabbit. It looked so out of place that it didn't seem real. Then it came to me that it could be play-acting - the two of them. He had given her the five pounds, and she was putting this on to get rid of me quickly.

But suddenly she slammed the door so hard in my face I could see how the glass in it came to be broken.

"Well, I don't want kids coming to my door!" she shouted at him on the other side. "Breaking the gate, breaking the windows, wearing out the path. How can I keep this place nice when I'm forever dragging to the door?"

She hit him then, I know she did. There was no play-acting about the bang as a foot hit the door, and Lenny yelling out loud as if a desk lid had come down on his head. But I didn't stop to hear any more. I'd heard enough to turn my stomach sick. Poor Lenny - I'd been worried about my mum and dad seeing him - and look what happened when his mum saw me! She had to be mad, that woman. And Lenny had to live with her! I didn't feel like crying, although my eyes had a hot rawness in them. More than anything, I just wanted to be back at home with my own family and the door shut tight.

Seeing my dad's car turn the corner was as if my dearest wish had been granted. He was going slowly, searching for me, with Nalini sitting up in front with big eyes. I waved and ran to them. I got in the back and I drew in my breath to tell them to go straight home. It was worth fifty pounds not to have them knocking at Lenny's house, never mind five. But they were too busy trying to speak to me.

"Have you been to the house? Did you say anything?"

"Yes, I've been to the house, but -"

"Did you accuse him?"

"No. I didn't get a chance -"

They both sat back in their seats, as if the car would drive itself home.

"Well, we must be grateful for that."

"We found the Postal Order."

I could hardly believe what my ears were hearing. *They had found the Postal Order.* Lenny hadn't taken it, after all!

"It wasn't in its envelope," Nalini was

saying. "He must have taken it out of that when he was tempted by it. But we can't accuse him of screwing up an envelope and hiding it in his pocket."

"No, no," I was saying, urging her to get on with things and tell me. "So where was it?"

"In with the Monopoly money. He couldn't put it back on the television, so he must have kept it in his pile of Monopoly money, and put it back in the box."

"Oh."

"Mum found it. In all the commotion after you went out she knocked the box off the chair, and when she picked the bits up, there was the Postal Order."

"It's certainly a good job you said nothing about it," my dad said. "And a good job I didn't telephone the police. We should have looked very small."

All I could think was how small I had felt, standing at Lenny's slammed door and hearing what his mother had said to him. And what about him getting beaten for having a friend call at his house?

My dad tried to be cheerful. "Anyway, who won?" he asked.

"Lenny won the Monopoly," I said.

In bed that night, I lay awake a long time,

thinking about it all. Lenny had taken some hard punishment from his mother. Some Red-Letter Day it had turned out to be! He would bear some hard thoughts about Prakash Patel.

He didn't come to school for a long time after that. But when he did, my heart sank into my boots. He came straight across the playground, the same flappy sleeves and dragging trouser bottoms, the same long, tangled hair - and he came straight for me. What would he do? Hit me? Spit in my face?

As he got close, I saw what was on his shirt, pinned there like a medal. It was his birthday badge.

"It's a good game, that Monopoly," he said out of the corner of his mouth. It was as if he was trying to tell me something.

"Yes," I said. "It's a good game all right."

I hadn't got the guts to tell him that I'd gone straight home that night and thrown it in the dustbin. Dealings with houses didn't appeal to me any more.

THE GREAT LEAPFROG CONTEST

BY WILLIAM SAROYAN

Rosie Mahoney was a tough little Irish kid whose folks, through some miscalculation in directions, or out of an innate spirit of anarchy, had moved into the Russian-Italian-and-Greek neighbourhood of my home town, across the Southern Pacific tracks, around G Street.

She wore a turtle-neck sweater, usually red. Her father was a bricklayer named Cull and a heavy drinker. Her mother's name was Mary. Mary Mahoney used to go to the Greek

Orthodox Catholic Church on Kearny Boulevard every Sunday, because there was no Irish Church to go to anywhere in the neighbourhood. The family seemed to be a happy one.

Rosie's three brothers had all grown up and gone to sea. Her two sisters had married. Rosie was the last of the clan. She had entered the world when her father had been close to sixty and her mother in her early fifties. For all that, she was hardly the studious or scholarly type.

Rosie had little use for girls, and as far as possible avoided them. She had less use for boys, but found it undesirable to avoid them. That is to say, she made it a point to take part in everything the boys did. She was always on hand, and always the first to take up any daring or crazy idea. Everybody felt awkward about her continuous presence, but it was no use trying to chase her away, because that meant a fight in which she asked no quarter, and gave none.

If she didn't whip every boy she fought, every fight was at least an honest draw, with a slight edge in Rosie's favour. She didn't fight girl-style, or cry if hurt. She fought the regular style and took advantage of every opening. It was very humiliating to be hurt by Rosie, so after a while any boy who thought of trying to chase her away, decided not to.

It was no use. She just wouldn't go. She didn't seem to like any of the boys especially, but she liked being in on any mischief they might have in mind, and she wanted to play on any teams they organized. She was an excellent baseball player, being as good as anybody else in the neighbourhood at any position, and for her age an expert pitcher. She had a wicked wing, too, and could throw a ball in from left fields so that when it hit the catcher's mitt it made a nice sound.

She was extraordinarily swift on her feet and played a beautiful game of tin-can hockey.

At pee-wee, she seemed to have the most disgusting luck in the world.

At the game we invented and used to call *Horse* she was as good at *horse* as at *rider*, and she insisted on following the rules of the game. She insisted on being horse when it was her turn to be horse. This always embarrassed her partner, whoever he happened to be, because it didn't seem right for a boy to be getting up on the back of a girl.

She was an excellent football player too.

As a matter of fact, she was just naturally

the equal of any boy in the neighbourhood, and much the superior of many of them. Especially after she had lived in the neighbourhood three years. It took her that long to make everybody understand that she had come to stay and that she was going to stay.

She did, too; even after the arrival of a boy named Rex Folger, who was from somewhere in the south of Texas. This boy Rex was a natural-born leader. Two months after his arrival in the neighbourhood, it was understood by everyone that if Rex wasn't the leader of the gang, he was very nearly the leader. He had fought and licked every boy in the neighbourhood who at one time or another had fancied himself leader. And he had done so without any noticeable ill-feeling, pride, or ambition.

As a matter of fact, no one could possibly have been more good-natured than Rex. Everybody resented him, just the same.

One winter, the whole neighbourhood took to playing a game that had become popular on the other side of the track, in another slum neighbourhood of the town: Leapfrog. The idea was for as many boys as cared to participate, to bend down and be leaped over by every other boy in the game, and then himself to get up and begin leaping over all the other boys, and then bend down again until all the boys had leaped over him again, and keep this up until all the other players had become exhausted. This didn't happen sometimes, until the last two players had travelled the distance of three or four miles, while the other players walked along, watching and making bets.

Rosie, of course, was always in on the game. She was always one of the last to drop out, too. And she was the only person in the neighbourhood Rex Folger hadn't fought and beaten.

He felt that that was much too humiliating even to think about. But inasmuch as she seemed to be a member of the gang, he felt that in some way or another he ought to prove his superiority.

One summer day during vacation, an argument between Rex and Rosie developed and Rosie pulled off her turtle-neck sweater and challenged him to a fight. Rex took a cigarette from his pocket, lit it, inhaled, and told Rosie he wasn't in the habit of hitting women - where he came from that amounted to boxing your mother. On the other hand, he said, if Rosie cared to compete with him in any other sport, he would be glad to oblige her. Rex was a very calm and courteous conversationalist. He had poise. It was unconscious, of course, but he had it just the same. He was just naturally a man who couldn't be hurried, flustered, or excited.

So Rex and Rosie fought it out in this game Leapfrog. They got to leaping over one another, quickly, too, until the first thing we knew the whole gang of us was out on the State Highway going south towards Fowler. It was a very hot day. Rosie and Rex were in great shape, and it looked like one was no tougher than the other nor more stubborn. They talked a good deal, especially Rosie, who insisted that she would have to fall down unconscious before she'd give up to a guy like Rex.

He said he was sorry his opponent was a girl. It grieved him deeply to have to make a girl exert herself to the point of death, but it was just too bad. He had to, so he had to. They leaped and squatted, leaped and squatted, and we got out to Sam Day's vineyard. That was halfway to Fowler. It didn't seem like either Rosie or Rex was ever going to get tired. They hadn't even begun to show signs of growing tired, although each of them was sweating a great deal.

Naturally, we were sure Rex would win the contest. But that was because we hadn't taken into account the fact that he was a simple person, whereas Rosie was crafty and shrewd. Rosie knew how to figure angles. She had discovered how to jump over Rex Folger in a way that weakened him. After a while, about three miles out of Fowler, we noticed that she was coming down on Rex's *neck*, instead of on his back. Naturally, this was hurting him and making the blood rush to his head. Rosie herself squatted in such a way that it was impossible, almost, for Rex to get anywhere near her neck with his hands.

Before long, we noticed that Rex was weakening. His head was getting closer and closer to the ground. About half a mile out of Fowler, we heard Rex's head bumping the ground every time Rosie leaped over him. They were good loud bumps that we knew were painful, but Rex wasn't complaining. He was too proud to complain.

Rosie, on the other hand, knew she had her man, and she was giving him all she had. She was bumping his head on the ground as solidly as she could, because she knew she didn't have much more fight in her, and if she didn't lay him out cold, in the hot sun, in the next ten minutes or so, she would fall down exhausted herself, and lose the contest.

Suddenly Rosie bumped Rex's head a real powerful one. He got up very dazed and very angry. It was the first time we had ever seen him fuming. By God, the girl was taking advantage of him, if he wasn't mistaken, and he didn't like it. Rosie was squatted in front of him. He came up groggy and paused a moment. Then he gave Rosie a very effective kick that sent her sprawling. Rosie jumped up and smacked Rex in the mouth. The gang jumped in and tried to establish order.

It was agreed that the Leapfrog contest must not change into a fight. Not any more. Not with Fowler only five or ten minutes away. The gang ruled further that Rex had had no right to kick Rosie and that in smacking him in the mouth Rosie had squared the matter, and the contest was to continue.

Rosie was very tired and sore; and so was Rex. They began leaping and squatting again; and again we saw Rosie coming down on Rex's neck so that his head was bumping the ground.

It looked pretty bad for the boy from Texas. We couldn't understand how he could take so much punishment. We all felt that Rex was getting what he had coming to him, but at the same time everybody seemed to feel badly about Rosie, a girl, doing the job instead of one of us. Of course, that was where we were wrong. Nobody but Rosie could have figured out that smart way of humiliating a very powerful and superior boy. It was probably the woman in her, which, less than five years later, came out to such an extent that she became one of the most beautiful girls in town, gave up her tomboy activities, and married one of the wealthiest young men in Kings County, a college man named, if memory serves, Wallace Hadington Finlay VI.

Less than a hundred yards from the heart of Fowler, Rosie, with great and admirable artistry, finished the job.

That was where the dirt of the highway siding ended and the paved main street of Fowler began. This street was paved with cement, not asphalt. Asphalt, in that heat, would have been too soft to serve, but cement had exactly the right degree of brittleness. I think Rex, when he squatted over the hard cement, knew the game was up. But he was brave to the end. He squatted over the hard cement and waited for the worst. Behind him, Rosie Mahoney prepared to make the supreme effort. In this next leap, she intended to give her all, which she did.

She came down on Rex Folger's neck like a ton of bricks. His head banged against the hard cement, his body straightened out, and his arms and legs twitched.

He was out like a light.

Six paces in front of him, Rosie Mahoney squatted and waited. Jim Telesco counted twenty, which was the time allowed for each leap. Rex didn't get up during the count.

The contest was over. The winner of the contest was Rosie Mahoney.

Rex didn't get up by himself at all. He just stayed where he was until a half-dozen of us lifted him and carried him to a horse trough, where we splashed water on his face.

Rex was a confused young man on the way back. He was also a deeply humiliated one. He couldn't understand anything about anything. He just looked dazed and speechless. Every now and then we imagined he wanted to talk, and I guess he did, but after we'd all gotten ready to hear what he had to say, he couldn't speak. He made a gesture so tragic that tears came to the eyes of eleven members of the gang.

Rosie Mahoney, on the other hand, talked all the way home. She said everything.

I think it made a better man of Rex. More

human. After that he was a gentler sort of soul. It may have been because he couldn't see very well for some time. At any rate, for weeks he seemed to be going around in a dream. His gaze would freeze on some insignificant object far away in the landscape, and half the time it seemed as if he didn't know where he was going, or why. He took little part in the activities of the gang, and the following winter he stayed away altogether. He came to school one day wearing glasses. He looked broken and pathetic.

That winter Rosie Mahoney stopped hanging around with the gang, too. She had a flair for making an exit at the right time.

THE MILE

BY GEORGE LAYTON

What a rotten report. It was the worst report I'd ever had. I'd dreaded bringing it home for my mum to read. We were sitting at the kitchen table having our tea, but neither of us had touched anything. It was gammon and chips as well, with a pineapple ring. My favourite. We have gammon every Friday, because my Auntie Doreen works on the bacon counter at the Co-op, and she drops it in on her way home. I don't think she pays for it.

My mum was reading the report for the third time. She put it down on the table and stared at me. I didn't say anything. I just stared at my gammon and chips and pineapple ring. What could I say? My mum looked so disappointed. I really felt sorry for her. She was determined for me to do well at school, and get my 'O' levels, then get my 'A' levels, then go to university, then get my degree, and then get a good job with good prospects…

"I'm sorry, Mum…"

She picked up the report again, and started reading it for the fourth time.

"It's no good reading it again, Mum. It's not going to get any better."

She slammed the report back on to the table.

"Don't you make cheeky remarks to me. I'm not in the mood for it!"

I hadn't meant it to be cheeky, but I suppose it came out like that.

"I wouldn't say anything if I was you, after reading this report!"

I shrugged my shoulders.

"There's nothing much I *can* say, is there?"

"You can tell me what went wrong. You told me you worked hard this term!"

I had told her I'd worked hard, but I hadn't.

"I did work hard, Mum."

"Not according to this."

She waved the report under my nose.

"You're supposed to be taking your O levels

next year. What do you think is going to happen then?"

I shrugged my shoulders again, and stared at my gammon and chips.

"I don't know."

She put the report back on the table. I knew I hadn't done well in my exams because of everything that had happened this term, but I didn't think for one moment I'd come bottom in nearly everything. Even Norbert Lightowler had done better than me.

"You've come bottom in nearly everything. Listen to this."

She picked up the report again.

"Maths - inattentive and lazy."

I knew what it said.

"I know what it says, Mum."

She leaned across the table, and put her face close to mine.

"I know what it says too, and I don't like it."

She didn't have to keep reading it.

"Well, stop reading it then."

My mum just gave me a look.

"English Language - he is capricious and dilettante. What does that mean?"

I turned the pineapple ring over with my fork. Oh heck, was she going to go through every rotten subject?

"Come on - English Language - Mr Melrose says you're 'capricious and dilettante'. What does he mean?"

"I don't know!"

I hate Melrose. He's really sarcarstic. He loves making a fool of you in front of other people. Well, he could stick his 'capricious and dilettante', and his rotten English Language, and his set books, and his horrible breath that nearly knocks you out when he stands over you.

"I don't know what he means."

"Well, you should know. That's why you study English Language, to understand words like that. It means you mess about and don't frame yourself."

My mum kept reading every part of the report over and over again. It was all so pointless. It wasn't as if reading it over and over again was going to change anything. Mind you, I kept my mouth shut. I just sat there staring at my tea. I knew her when she was in this mood.

"What I can't understand is how come you did so well at Religious Instruction. You got seventy-five percent."

I couldn't understand that either.

"I like Bible stories, Mum." She wasn't sure if I was cheeking her or not. I wasn't.

"Bible stories? It's all I can do to get you to come to St. Cuthbert's one Sunday a month with me and your Auntie Doreen."

That was true, but what my mum didn't know was that the only reason I went was because my Auntie Doreen slips me a few bob!

"And the only reason you go then is because your Auntie Doreen gives you pocket money."

"Aw, that's not true, Mum."

Blimey! My mum's got eyes everywhere.

She put the report back into the envelope. Hurray! The Spanish Inquisition was over. She took it out again. Trust me to speak too soon.

"I mean, you didn't even do well at sport, did you? 'Sport - he is not a natural athlete.' Didn't you do *anything* right this term?"

I couldn't help smiling to myself. No, I'm not a natural athlete, but I'd done one thing right this term. I'd shown Arthur Boocock that he couldn't push me around any more. That's why everything else had gone wrong. That's why I was 'lazy and inattentive' at Maths, and 'capricious and dilettante' at

English Language. That's why this last term had been so miserable, because of Arthur blooming Boocock.

He'd only come into our class this year because he'd been kept down. I didn't like him. He's a right bully, but because he's a bit older and is good at sport and running and things, everybody does what he says.

That's how Smokers' Corner started.

Arthur used to pinch his dad's cigarettes and bring them to school, and we'd smoke them at playtime in the shelter under the woodwork classroom. We called it Smokers' Corner.

It was daft really. I didn't even like smoking, it gives me headaches. But I joined in because all the others did. Well, I didn't want Arthur Boocock picking on me.

We took it in turns to stand guard. I liked it when it was my turn, it meant I didn't have to join in the smoking.

Smokers' Corner was at the top end of the playground, opposite the girls' school. That's how I first saw Janis. It was one playtime. I was on guard, when I saw these three girls staring at me from an upstairs window. They kept laughing and giggling. I didn't take much notice, which was a good job because I saw

57

Melrose coming aross the playground with Mr Rushton, the deputy head. I ran into the shelter and warned the lads.

"Arthur, Tony - Melrose and Rushton are coming!"

There was no way we could've been caught. We knew we could get everything away before Melrose or Rushton or anybody could reach us, even if they ran across the playground as fast as they could. We had a plan you see.

First, everybody put their cigarettes out, but not on the ground, with your fingers. It didn't half hurt if you didn't wet them enough. Then Arthur would open a little iron door that was in the wall next to the boiler house. Norbert found it ages ago. It must've been there for years. Tony reckoned it was some sort of oven. Anyway, we'd empty our pockets and put all the cigarettes inside. All the time we'd be waving our hands about to get rid of the smoke, and Arthur would squirt the fresh-air spray he'd nicked from home. Then we'd shut the iron door and start playing football or tig.

Melrose never let on why he used to come storming across the playground. He never said anything, but we knew he was trying to catch the Smokers, and he knew we knew. All he'd do was give us all a look in turn, and march off. But on that day, the day those girls had been staring and giggling at me, he did say something.

"Watch it! All of you. I know what you're up to. Just watch it. Specially you, Boocock."

We knew why Melrose picked on Arthur Boocock.

"You're running for the school on Saturday, Boocock. You'd better win or I'll want to know the reason why."

Mr Melrose is in charge of athletics, and Arthur holds the school record for the mile. Melrose reckons he could run for Yorkshire one day if he trains hard enough.

I didn't like this smoking lark, it made me cough, gave me a headache, and I was sure we'd get caught one day.

"Hey, Arthur, we'd better pack it in. Melrose is going to catch us one of these days."

Arthur wasn't bothered.

"Ah you! You're just scared, you're yeller!"

Yeah, I was blooming scared.

"I'm not. I just think he's going to catch us."

Then Arthur did something that really shook me. He took his right hand out of his blazer pocket. For a minute I thought he was going to hit me, but he didn't. He put it to his mouth instead, and blew out some smoke. He's mad. He'd kept his cigarette in his hand in his pocket all the time. He's mad. I didn't say anything though. I was scared he'd thump me.

On my way home after school that day, I saw those girls. They were standing outside Wilkinson's sweetshop, and when they saw me they started giggling again. They're daft, girls. They're always giggling. One of them, the tallest, was ever so pretty though. The other two were all right, but not as pretty as the tall girl. It was the other two that were doing most of the giggling.

"Go on, Glenda, ask him."

"No, you ask him."

"No, you're the one who wants to know. You ask him."

"Shurrup!"

The tall one looked as embarrassed as I felt. I could see her name written on her school-bag: Janis Webster.

The other two were still laughing, and telling each other to ask me something. I could feel myself going red. I didn't like being stared at.

"Do you two want a photograph or summat?"

They giggled even more.

No thank you, we don't collect photos of monkeys, do we, Glenda?"

The one called Glenda stopped laughing and gave the other one a real dirty look.

"Don't be so rude, Christine."

Then this Christine started teasing her friend Glenda.

"Ooh, just because you like him, Glenda Bradshaw, just because you fancy him."

I started walking away. Blimey! If any of the lads came by and heard this going on, I'd never hear the end of it. The one called Christine started shouting after me.

"Hey my friend Glenda thinks you're ever so nice. She wants to know if you want to go out with her."

Blimey! Why did she have to shout so the whole street could hear? I looked round to make sure nobody like Arthur Boocock or Norbert or Tony were about. I didn't want them to hear these stupid lasses saying things like that. I mean, we didn't go out with girls, because… well, we just didn't.

I saw the pretty one, Janis, pulling Christine's arm. She was telling her to stop embarrassing me. She was nice that Janis, much nicer than the other two. I mean, if I was forced to go out with a girl, you know if somebody said, "You will die tomorrow if you don't go out with a girl", then I wouldn't have minded going out with Janis Webster. She was really nice.

I often looked out for her after that, but when I saw her, she was always with the other two. The one time I did see her on her own, I was walking home with Tony and Norbert and I pretended I didn't know her, even though she smiled and said hello. Of course, I sometimes used to see her at playtime, when it was my turn to stand guard at Smokers' Corner. I liked being on guard twice as much now. As well as not having to smoke, it gave me a chance to see Janis. She was smashing. I couldn't get her out of my mind. I was always thinking about her, you know, having daydreams. I was forever 'rescuing' her.

One of my favourite rescues was where she was being bullied by about half-a-dozen lads, not hitting her or anything, just mucking about. And one of them was always Arthur Boocock. And I'd go up very quietly and say "Are these lads bothering you?" And before she had time to answer, a fight would start, and I'd take them all on. All six at once, and it would end up with them pleading for mercy.

And then Janis would put her hand on my arm and ask me to let them off... and I would. That was my favourite rescue.

That's how the trouble with Arthur Boocock started.

I'd been on guard one playtime, and had gone into one of my 'rescues'. It was the swimming-bath rescue. Janis would be swimming in the deep end, and she'd get into trouble, and I'd dive in and rescue her. I'd bring her to the side, put a towel round her, and then walk off without saying a word. Bit daft really, because I can't swim. Not a stroke. Mind you, I don't suppose I could beat up six lads on my own either, especially if one of them was Arthur Boocock. Anyway, I was just pulling Janis out of the deep end when I heard Melrose shouting his head off.

"Straight to the Headmaster's study. Go on, all three of you!"

I looked round, and I couldn't believe it. Melrose was inside Smoker's Corner. He'd caught Arthur, Tony and Norbert. He was giving Arthur a right crack over the head. How had he caught them? I'd been there all the time... standing guard... thinking about Janis... I just hadn't seen him coming... oh heck...

"I warned you, Boocock, all of you. Go and report to the Headmaster!"

As he was going past me, Arthur showed me his fist. I knew what that meant.

They all got the cane for smoking, and Melrose had it in for Arthur even though he was still doing well at his running. The more Melrose picked on Arthur, the worse it was for me, because Arthur kept beating me up.

That was the first thing he'd done after he'd got the cane - beaten me up. He reckoned I'd not warned them about Melrose on purpose.

"How come you didn't see him? He's blooming big enough."

"I just didn't"

I couldn't tell him that I'd been daydreaming about Janis Webster.

"He must have crept up behind me."

Arthur hit me, right on my ear.

"How could he go behind you? You had your back to the wall. You did it on purpose, you yeller-belly!"

And he hit me again, on the same ear.

After that, Arthur hit me every time he saw me. Sometimes, he'd hit me in the stomach, sometimes on the back of the neck. Sometimes, he'd raise his fist and I'd think he was going to hit me, and he'd just walk away laughing. Then he started taking my spending money. He'd say, "Oh, you don't want that, do you?" and I'd say, "No, you have it, Arthur."

I was really scared of him. He made my life a misery. I dreaded going to school, and when I could, I'd stay at home by pretending to be poorly. I used to stick my fingers down my throat and make myself sick.

I suppose that's when I started to get behind with my school work, but anything was better than being bullied by that rotten Arthur Boocock. And when I did go to school, I'd try to stay in the classroom at playtime, or I'd make sure I was near the teacher who was on playground duty. Of course, Arthur thought it was all very funny, and he'd see if he could hit me without the teacher seeing, which he could.

Dinner time was the worst because we had an hour free before the bell went for school dinners, and no one was allowed to stay inside. It was a school rule. That was an hour for Arthur to bully me. I used to try and hide but he'd always find me.

By now it didn't seem to have anything to do with him being caught smoking and getting the cane. He just seemed to enjoy hitting me and tormenting me. So I stopped going to school dinners. I used to get some chips, or a Cornish pasty, and wander around. Sometimes I'd go into town and look at the shops, or else I'd go in the park and muck about. Anything to get away from school and Arthur Boocock.

That's how I met Archie.

There's a running track in the park, a proper one with white lines and everything, and one day I spent all dinner time watching this old bloke running round. That was Archie. I went back the next day and he was there again, running round and round, and I got talking to him.

"Hey, mister, how fast can you run a mile?"

I was holding a bag of crisps, and he came over and took one. He grinned at me.

"How fast can *you* run a mile?"

I'd never tried running a mile.

"I don't know, I've never tried."

He grinned again.

"Well, now's your chance. Come on, get your jacket off."

He was ever so fast and I found it hard to keep up with him, but he told me I'd done well. I used to run with Archie every day after that. He gave me an old track-suit top, and I'd change into my shorts and trainers and chase round the track after him. Archie said I was getting better and better.

"You'll be running for Yorkshire one of these days."

I laughed and told him to stop teasing me. He gave me half an orange. He always did after running.

"Listen, lad, I'm serious. It's all a matter of training. Anybody can be good if they train hard enough. See you tomorrow."

That's when I got the idea.

I decided to go in for the mile in the school sports at the end of term. You had to be picked for everything else, but anybody could enter the mile.

There were three weeks to the end of term, and in that three weeks I ran everywhere. I ran to school. I ran with Archie every dinner time. I went back and ran on the track after school. Then I'd run home. If my mum wanted anything from the shops, I'd run there. I'd get up early in the mornings and run before breakfast. I was always running. I got into tons of trouble at school for not doing my homework properly, but I didn't care. All I thought about was the mile.

I had daydreams about it. Always me and

Arthur, neck and neck, and Janis would be cheering me on. Then I dropped Janis from my daydreams. She wasn't important any more. It was just me and Arthur against each other. I was sick of him and his bullying.

Arthur did well at sports day. He won the high jump and the long jump. He was picked for the half mile and the four-forty, and won them both. Then there was the announcement for the mile.

"Will all those competitors who wish to enter the open mile please report to Mr Melrose at the start."

I hadn't let on to anybody that I was going to enter, so everybody was very surprised to see me when I went over in my shorts and trainers - especially Melrose. Arthur thought it was hilarious.

"Well, look who it is. Do you want me to give you half a mile start?"

I ignored him, and waited for Melrose to start the race. I surprised a lot of people that day, but nobody more than Arthur. I stuck to him like a shadow. When he was forward, I went forward. If he dropped back, I dropped back. This went on for about half the race. He kept giving me funny looks. He couldn't understand what was happening.

"You won't keep this up. Just watch."

And he suddenly spurted forward. I followed him, and when he looked round to see how far ahead he was, he got a shock when he saw he wasn't.

It was just like my daydreams. Arthur and me, neck and neck, the whole school cheering us on, both of us heading for the last bend. I looked at Arthur and saw the tears rolling down his cheeks. He was crying his eyes out. I knew at that moment I'd beaten him. I don't mean I knew I'd won the race. I wasn't bothered about that. I knew I'd beaten *him*, Arthur. I knew he'd never hit me again.

That's when I walked off the track. I didn't see any point in running the last two hundred yards. I suppose that's because I'm not a natural athlete...

"'Sport - he is not a natural athlete.' Didn't you do anything right this term?"

Blimey! My mum was still reading my report. I started to eat my gammon and chips. They'd gone cold.

DUFFINGS

BY E.W. HILDICK

It had to happen. From the very first day he came to spend his holidays in the village and I'd twitted him for his fancy Southern accent, and he'd punched me in the teeth, and I'd hit him back, and we'd gone on and on and on in the bottom of Church Field until all we could do in response to the cheers and jeers was stand glaring at each other, fists up, and trying not to cry - since that day, my leadership had been in question and I wanted it sorting out. I knew that in four weeks' time he'd be going back home and there'd be an end of this "What's David think?" or "What's David going to do?" whenever I suggested anything.

But four weeks is a long time...

So at last, after two or three days, I threw out a challenge. I knew fighting was no good, so I challenged him to the next best thing: Duffings.

"How about a game of duffings on the cut-side?" I suggested, this damp afternoon, just after tea, when the grass was too wet for cricket. We were sitting on the graveyard wall with a handful of chippings each, trying to hit the garden-party notice.

"Naargh! Let's go fishing! David said he'd like to do a bit of fishing some day."

Here we go, I thought... I could have booted little Poppy Hopkin clean off the wall.

"Duffings!" I said, very firm.

"What *is* duffings?" asked David.

I looked at him and thought how much I hated his little boy hair - straight brushed forward with a bit of a fringe - and his beauty spot under his left eye, and his khaki shorts, and his lah-de-posh accent.

"Duffings," I said. "Not daffings... Duffings is, well... duffings..."

Jud Cartright chipped in:

"When you come to something and dare the others to do it. That's what -"

"Look, lad," I said, leaning forward and

71

poking his chest. "David was asking me what duffings is, not you! You just keep quiet or you'll find your nice new Grammar School cap in Pearson's pond, yonder..." I turned to David. "Duffings is when you duff when someone tells you to do summat and you daren't, after they've already done it themselves. It's counted against you. Then it's your turn to do sumat you *dare* do, and if *they* duff it's counted against *them*."

"It's a daft game! Let's go fishing."

I gave Poppy a look.

"It's only daft because you always get most points against you! Well, what about it, David? Just me and you. These two can keep score. Course, if *you're* a bit scared, too..."

He slid off the wall, dusted his pants and said:

"Let's go!"

I saw Poppy wink at Jud and I knew they were dying for David to show me up, but I wasn't bothered. I'd a few good tests up my sleeve.

The first was on the way to the cut, passing Pearson's farmyard.

"See that dog?" I said, pointing to a big shaggy black and white sheep-dog leaping up in its chains and barking. "I'm going over this gate and I'm gonner pat its head while you lot count five."

And over I went, with the dog nearly going crackers, nearly striking sparks out of its chain, and as I went up to it I kept muttering, "Good dog, good dog! What is it then, eh, lad, what's up, eh…?"

Of course, I knew it wasn't as bad as it sounded and I'd used it for my first duffing so many times I reckon it knew me as well as Edgar Pearson himself. But it looked hard, me patting it gently while it growled and slavered and rolled its eyes and lifted its lip up - and I smiled, thinking how David would be sweating on the top line, already, first go off.

Then when the others had reached five, I moved over a bit so they couldn't see, and instead of giving it a nice quiet pat to finish with, I let it have a smart little crack on top of its nose, just to liven it up a bit.

"You cracked it one! You cracked it one! Foul! You allus do that! Foul go! Doesn't count!"

Poppy had been standing on the wall, watching. I grabbed his ankles and asked him if he wanted me to pull him down and roll him in the muck. I gave him a tug and he screamed. Then I let him go and turned to see

73

how David was getting on.

He was smiling - a bit shaky, I thought. But he pushed back his fringe and went over the gate. And he knew about talking all the time, too, and he stood there patting the dog long past five…

One thing in my favour, I'll admit, was that David wasn't used either to the game or the countryside. He threw his first turn away by climbing on to a wall and running along from the corner of a field to the gate. It was dead easy, but it gave me an idea. I did the same a bit faster, and when I got to the gate I carried on and jumped to the wall at the other side and told him to get on with that.

Well, he got a bit of a graze on his right shin but he did it.

"The next best place we come to is the old canal," I said. "Just past those corn stacks there and to the right, down the field. I'd save your turn till we get there if I was you."

Up piped Poppy: "Nowt o' the sort! Foul! You just dare him to walk in and out between the stacks, Dave!"

I was so mad I could have throttled him. But I daren't show it. I tried to laugh it off by saying that David would waste his turn if he dared me to walk in and out of some old corn ricks. Then Jud butted in and told him not to believe me and that was the one thing they always got a point for when they were playing Duffings with me.

David was looking puzzled.

"But what's daring about it?"

Poppy stretched his mouth wide and stared at me.

"Rats! Rat-ricks! Look, stop a minute and sniff up! You can smell 'em from here!"

Poppy and Jud weren't half grinning. I tried not to shiver as they took it in turns to rub it in.

"Crawlin' all over!"

"Squeaking at you!"

"Fair feel their tails tickling your neck when you go between the stacks!"

David was laughing. We'd just about reached the things by now and I'd got my hands tight in my pockets.

"Yes," he said. "I think I *will* have a little stroll round. Shall I bring one out to shake hands with you?"

And off he went round all that rustling straw, whistling as merry as you like. And that was definitely one to him.

By the time we reached the canal I was feeling as wild as Edgar Pearson's dog, they kept on so long about the rats. David didn't say much himself, but while the others kept making their cracks he smiled so quiet and superior that I felt maddest of the lot at him.

"Right, lad!" I thought. "You just wait, lad! I'll knock that smirk off your face!"

But I soon found out it wasn't going to be so easy.

When I walked on the parapet of the hump-backed bridge backwards, from one side to the other - he did the same. And when he followed this up by hopping on the parapet instead of walking, I'd a job to do it myself. Same when I stood with my shoes and socks off in the weeds at the edge and sank up to my knees in the mud while the others counted ten - he did it too, without panicking for someone to grab him like Poppy would have done. "Now *you* do *this*!" he said, going back to near the bridge, where the bank was firmly bricked up. And he did a handstand, right at the edge, and waved his bare legs about, all wet and muddy, while we counted another ten. Luckily I was pretty good at handstands, but I must say it isn't so nice doing them with the knowledge you'll get a ducking if you overbalance.

At the old locks it was the same. We swung,

balanced, hopped, hung and jumped. We went over, under, along, up and down the rotten splintered gates. And although I always managed to do what he did, not once could I get him to duff.

So he was still one up, and Jud and Poppy weren't half David-ing it, when I decided now or never, once and for all, one last chance, on the pylon. You never know, I thought. Just as I can't stand rats, he might not like heights. It was another of those things.

Now this pylon stood in a field at the back of the remains of the lock-keeper's cottage. It was one of a line of new pylons they were putting up and it was still without cables.

"Well," I said, "we'll leave the canal for a bit now, and we'll try a new one." I pointed to the tower, gleaming white against some bruise-coloured clouds. "I'm gonner climb that!"

I was watching his face. I thought he turned a bit pale. But he still kept up that toffee-nosed smiling.

"Suits me."

"To the top!"

"Fair enough."

When I came to climb the little peg things that stuck out I found they were big steel bolts set wide apart. They were fairly easy to manage and they made you go up in big strides, and I was beginning to think that maybe this was one of the easiest of the lot when I looked down and got a shock to see how far up I was. Jud and Poppy and David were staring up, three white blobs; the canal was just a line of bushes; the village a cluster of stone boxes in the distance.

Then I looked up and saw I wasn't half way to the top, and this made me feel a bit worried. If it seemed so high this far, I thought - as I climbed another couple of pegs - what would it be like up there?

I stopped for another look down. It was getting quite breezy but it wasn't keeping me from sweating. My hands felt slippery.

"You all right up there?"

It was David's voice. I thought at first he was mocking me, but then it came up again, thin and high and anxious.

I was going to shout back but somehow I couldn't think what to say. My hands were really wet now. I was going to wipe them on my shirt, one at a time. I wondered which to let go with first, but again my mind didn't seem to be able to work properly and I couldn't decide. Then Jud said something about coming down and it wasn't worth it and I looked down again and things seemed to spin. I leaned forward, pressing my body into the slats and struts, glad to feel their hard cold edges on my flesh. My ears were roaring and swishing like sea-shell...

"Stay there... stay there... stay there..."

Through the swishing came this voice.

It was comforting to feel the chest and shoulders of someone else, firm against my thighs, pinning me. And gradually, as I felt my confidence come back, I was able to flex my left foot, which had gone numb where I'd jammed it in the angle of a strut. Then I eased my right foot, rubbing it along the bolt it stood on, and I wondered if there was a groove in the instep. But I didn't look down. And I didn't look up. I kept my eyes shut.

"When you're ready," came the voice. "But take your time."

I smiled. I felt light-headed and wanted to chatter to show how I'd been in a nasty fix but was all right now, perfectly all right, quite safe, glad to be alive... I said:

"All right! Let's go... And this can count for your turn, David... You've won..."

I eased myself down a step. The other boy moved with me. We paused. Then we went down another… and another…

"Nearly there?… Good!…"

I jumped the last few feet and sat down on the grass, glad to feel it.

"Gosh! Are you OK?"

David was white now and no mistake. Really white, all round the mouth.

"Not bad," I said, wondering how to thank him without making it sound mushy.

"Well, that's a point to you! I wouldn't do it now for a thousand quid!"

I looked up at him.

"But I said up there…"

"You said all sorts up there, lad! You were even calling me David!"

I stared at Poppy.

"What? *You*?"

Jud put an arm on Poppy's shoulder.

"Aye! Poppy!"

I rubbed my hands on the grass. After a while I said: "It's dry enough for cricket after all."

David shrugged. His colour had come back.

"Yes… But I'd thought about getting our bikes out and…"

"What's *Poppy* think?" said Jud.

"Fishing!"

So fishing we all went.

CLEO THE VIGILANT

BY TIM KENNEMORE

"And so in the end I spent the night in the bath," said Katie, "and I never did find my socks."

Gina chuckled, sticking her finger in and out of the wire netting that was such an intrinsic part of the decor of the Girls' Cloakroom. It took very little imagination to feel that you were actually in the monkey house at the Zoo: the passage down the side (for visitors); the netting dividing the room into rectangular compartments. Far right: First Years (gibbon) followed by Seconds (Barbary ape), Thirds (marmoset), Fourths...

"Katie - someone coming!" hissed Gina in sudden panic. They froze, looking wildly around for some means of escape. There were no means of escape. Not even a coat to hide behind - the coats were all outside on their shivering owners. Which was where Katie and Gina were supposed to be. And in they came, before Katie had time to throw herself to the floor and pretend to be having a fit. In came the prefects.

They entered in formation: in a perfect V like the Red Arrows. And in the leading position, at the apex of the V, Cleo Langham. It couldn't have been worse.

"Right! What do you think you're doing indoors? I'm sick and tired of this insolence from the lower school. You know perfectly well you aren't allowed in until the bell." Little angry red spots appeared on Cleo Langham's Persil Automatic whiter-than-white cheeks. The dots looked clownish. "Blatant! Caught red-handed!" You'd think they'd been vandalizing the school building at the very least. "Now out. And consider yourselves lucky I'm not giving you an order mark. But if I ever catch you two in here again..." She folded her arms. The two behind her promptly folded theirs, too, mixed expressions of dislike and enjoyment flickering over their anonymous, pinched, nonentity prefect faces. Whatever people had looked like in the fifth year, promotion and the prefect tie seemed to do that to them. Their faces changed subtly to fit the mould. Not so Cleo Langham. Her appearance totally belied her nature. Long blonde hair, perfect cameo features in a delicate round face, ivory skin. Only in the pale blue icy eyes was there a clue. Those eyes looked as though they fired lasers. But otherwise - the face of an angel, and the nature of a particularly tyrannical dictator. There was a joke in the third year that Cleo Langham was campaigning for prefects to be armed with sub-machine guns, and given permission to shoot on sight. She'd enjoy that, would Cleo.

"Move!"

They got to their feet. It would certainly have been wisest to exit, shamefaced and speechless, with all possible speed. But this was not Katie's nature. "It's terribly cold out, you know," she said. "Said on the radio it might snow, later."

"Tough," said Cleo. The flunkeys nodded; well said, Cleo. "Won't do you any harm. Nobody ever died of the cold."

This was so plainly ridiculous that Katie couldn't help laughing, although she knew full well what a perilous thing this was to do. "Scott of the Antarctic," she said. "Captain Oates," she added hopefully.

"Don't be cheeky!" One mustn't contradict. If Cleo says that the world is square, start looking for the corners. "Now get out!"

"C'mon," muttered Gina, sensing that Katie was in one of her whimsical, hell-to-the-consequences moods. These were most dangerous. And she was right; as they reached the cloakroom door, their every movement closely watched as if they might produce hand grenades from their coat pockets, Katie hesitated, then turned as if propelled by some force she was powerless to resist, looked Cleo Langham straight in the eye and said, conversationally:

"I think that I shall never see, a prefect uglier than thee."

There was an ominous silence - Gina battling to supress an explosion of laughter, Katie's eyes sparkling with dread and delight, Cleo standing there in stunned disbelief, while the flunkeys gaped, and exchanged expectant glances. "Right!" hissed Cleo, finally. "Detention! Gross disrespect! And you..." she glared at Gina... "can have an order mark." This seemed rather hard, but one does not expect justice from Cleo Langham. Out came the little notebook. "Name and form?"

"Sharon Vaughan, 3H," said Katie.

"Oh, you're Sharon Vaughan, are you? I've heard of you. And you?"

"Lucy Connell," said Katie for Gina, who seemed lost for words. Cleo, apparently, considered this quite natural. People should be speechless with awe, in the terrible presence of Cleo Langham. "Now get out."

Out they went. It was cold - bitter, biting cold and still ten minutes before the bell. They set off to walk round the Science Block. If you stood still on a morning like this you'd probably freeze fast to the ground and they'd have to come and hack you away, and take you indoors to melt.

"And what's Sharon Vaughan going to say, when she finds out about that?" Gina banged her gloved hands together, and watched as her breath steamed off into a little cloud.

"She gets so many detentions, she won't even notice one more," said Katie. "And even if she did, she'd be pleased. She'd thank me. She's trying to get herself expelled, didn't you know that?"

"No…"

Gina didn't really know Sharon Vaughan at all; she was a dark, hefty girl, in a different form from herself and Katie. Katie, however, knew her well; they lived in the same road.

"She can't stand it here. She plays truant half the time. She reckons if they kick her out she'll be able to go to Kendall Lane. She wanted to go there all along. So did I."

"So did I," said Gina, stamping on a tiny frozen puddle. The ice shattered with a crunch; water oozed out murkily. "Nobody at junior school wanted to come to Compton Park. It was the parents."

"Oh, parents think it's fantastic," said Katie crossly, "this stupid uniform, and lots of discipline and *prefects*. They haven't got to come here, have they? We do. And naturally nobody asks us. What we think isn't *relevant*. *Bloody* Cleo Langham," she added, kicking the ground in sudden temper. "Going on about cheek and that. Gross disrespect. She's only three years older than me! Why should I have any respect for her, her with the manners of a pig?"

"Don't be insulting to pigs," said Gina. "Pigs are nice." Gina was always a stout defender of the pig. She believed it to be a much maligned animal, and refused to eat it in any form.

"Quite right," said Katie. "Gross disrespect," she muttered again. "There's only one of me. It takes a hundred and forty-four people, gross disrespect does."

"You'll end up doing Maths O Level yet," said Gina. "No, really though, the way they go on as if they've actually done something, been chosen for some great honour. All you've got to do is survive to the Sixth form to be a prefect."

"It's bribery," said Katie. "Hooper's way of getting people to stay on. Everyone knows she gets more money, for every sixth former. So they get this reward, being a prefect. And that looks good on their college applications and things. It's all *corrupt*. You scratch my back, I'll scratch yours." Simultaneously, they burst into giggles, picturing Cleo Langham scratching Mrs Hooper's back. "A little bit to the right dear," gasped Katie, trying to do Mrs Hooper's voice through her laughter. "Ah *that's* the spot! Oh bliss!"

And then the bell went, and they staggered through the north end main door, under the suspicious eye of the trio of prefects who guarded it from inside, in the warm.

As they headed for their own cloakroom, Gina sobered up. It was all very well for Katie to say that about Sharon not minding, but what about Lucy Connell? It wasn't as if Gina wasn't involved. Katie's high spirits and seemingly uncontrollable tongue often lead to trouble, but it was generally very minor trouble. This might be serious. Cleo was sure to find out, sooner or later, and probably sooner, who Katie Walker was, or, more likely, who Sharon Vaughan was. She said something of this to Katie.

"Course she won't," said Katie. "And if she does, she won't remember. It'll be just a name, that she's given a detention to at some time. You know Cleo. By the end of every single day she's got a list of order marks and detentions long as your arm. They all blend into a sort of blur: filthy juniors. I bet she's given Sharon loads of order marks already. She said she knew the name; that'll be why. And she didn't remember that it wasn't me, did she? As long as nothing happens in the next day or two we're safe as anything. You worry too much, you do, Gina Bionic Window Cleaner."

"Um," said Gina, somewhat comforted.

Katie was probably right - she nearly always was. The only thing - what if Sharon Vaughan, the real one, was to cross Cleo's horrible path, within the next day or two, the danger period? They hadn't any control over that, had they? Still, it was a very big school, Compton Park... and Sharon was more than likely off playing truant.

Their formroom was on the ground floor, just down the corridor from the main hall. This had both good points and bad. It meant you could be first in the queue for snacks at break, and you didn't have to do the Great Trek every morning to get to Assembly. The bad bit was that people were always passing. You were Observed.

Cathy Mitchell was standing outside the door, which was half open. "Watch it," she said. "Simon Dixon's just behind the door, and he's pulling all the girls' skirts up as we go in."

"Ta," said Katie. "Amazing what some people'll do for an eyeful of navy knicker. Retarded." She stepped forward and gave the door a might kick. It flew back; there was a howl. "Stupid sort of place to stand, innit, Dixon?" she said, strolling in. "Get hurt, standing there." Roars of delight from the class. Simon Dixon was clutching his funny bone; he eyed Katie with loathing. "May as well have the leg to match it," said Katie, and kicked him in the shin. Cheers of derision. In came Miss Fleming.

"Will you all go to your seats please. Dixon, get up this minute. You'll make the floor dirty. Now, I want everyone to listen carefully, and the girls in particular." She perched herself on the front of the table. Miss Fleming hated sitting in her chair; she would wander around, lean against the wall, balance herself on the chair arm; anything but sit in it. "There's been another outbreak of this ridiculous behaviour in the girls' toilets. All the toilets jammed up with toilet rolls again. Shut up, Harper, that's not funny. Now, I'm asking you for the last time. Does anybody in this form know anything about it?" Silence. "I'm not suggesting anyone here is responsible. I'm sure you know better than that. But it's quite possible that you might know, or have a pretty good idea, just who is doing it. And it's essential that the culprits are caught. Mrs Hooper doesn't see why anyone should have the bother of unblocking the toilets every night, so until further notice the toilets are out of bounds expect during break and lunchtime, when there will be prefects there, supervising. During lesson-time they will be locked."

"Oh, Miss Fleming." Groans from all the girls. "But sometimes you have to go during a lesson."

"Thank you, Lindy, I hadn't finished. In cases of emergency you ask one of the staff for permission to use the sixth form toilets. Understood? Good. And you boys needn't look so pleased with yourselves. There have been plenty of incidents of vandalism in the boys' toilets, and Mrs Hooper is quite prepared to introduce the same measures for you. So if anyone does know anything, they'd do well to report it. Otherwise everyone's going to suffer. Right. Now I'll take the register."

She did this standing, leaning against the wall, one foot resting on the pipes.

"That's a bit much," said Gina to Kate. "Who on earth can be doing that? Sharon Vaughan?"

"Dunno. It's a bit mental, stuffing loo paper down toilets. Sharon's not mental. She hasn't said anything about it. If it was her she'd have got herself caught by now, probably. The whole point of what she's doing, is getting caught."

"Who then?"

"Perhaps that Michelle Wicks and her lot. You know, that Second Year with the fuzzy hair, got herself suspended last term. I reckon it might be her. They'll never find out. They'll keep this up for a few days, that's all. Then it'll be something else. I dunno though, prefects in the bog. Imagine, nature calling like crazy, and Cleo Langham outside, supervising. Instant constipation. Ugh."

"Bet that'll thrill them to death, though," said Gina. "Being stuck in the loos during break and all through lunch. They'll really enjoy that."

"Serve 'em right," said Katie. "Oh heck, I haven't packed my stuff yet. What's first lesson? Oh, Maths. Good."

But first, out to Assembly, with prefects lining all the corridors and intersections, bawling their parrot-like cries: "Stop talking! Shut up! *Will* you stop talking?" The prefects made such a row that if they shut up themselves and left the rest of the school to it, the resulting noise would probably be no worse, thought Gina. If *she* ran a school she'd want it to be a happy place. This was like going to a daily early morning funeral. Dead

Silence. What harm would a little quiet chatter do? Rules for the sake of rules.

When the holy bits were over Mrs Hooper rose, majestically, to do her announcements. She announced, through her crackling microphone, that Mrs Harrison would be leaving at the end of term. Ripples of indifference ran around the hall. They would, continued Mrs Hooper balefully, be *very sorry to lose her*. Gina didn't even know who she was. So many teachers, and most of them you never had anything to do with at all. Grimly, Mrs Hooper went on to repeat what Miss Fleming had said about the girls' toilets, and to give her opinion of such infantile behaviour. "And that is all I have to say. Stand!" Like the flipping army, stand, sit, turn. "Turn! And lead on." The school filed out, under the ever-watchful eyes of the prefects. And their mouths. "Shut up!" Stuart Burnford roared at Katie.

"But I didn't say anything," she complained, in the safety of the formroom. "I only got as far as opening my mouth. I might have been going to cough, or *breathe* or something."

"No breathing in the corridors!" said Gina. Stuart Burnford was a giant-sized rat. He was the male equivalent of Cleo Langham, except that he had the face to fit his character: a prize fighter's mug, with a handful of nasty little pimples tastefully scattered. He and Cleo Langham were going out together. They were even rumoured to be getting engaged.

"Imagine what it'll be like for their kids, if they ever have any," Katie said, as they made their way to Room 5 and Maths. "They'll never let them in the house. 'Mummy, please can I come in for my tea?' 'No! Outside!'"

Gina giggled. "'Daddy, I'm so cold and it's nearly two in the morning, can't I please come in to bed?'" "'No!'" they chorused. "'Outside!'"

"They'll spend their entire married life," said Katie, "stationed one at the back door, one at the front, seeing that the kids don't get indoors..."

"Till one of them rings a bell." This picture of the future Langham/Burnford menage was almost unbearably funny; they half-collapsed into their desks.

"You two, you're always laughing at something," said Vicky Watts, somewhat enviously, turning round from the seat in front.

"I suppose we are," said Katie, weakly. "Oh

dear..." and she was off again. Vicky waited, but, clearly, the joke was not to be explained to her; she shrugged, turned back, and proceeded to be very nasty indeed to her friend Julie, for being so dull and unamusing.

"Where's our Adam got to?" asked Katie. "How'm I supposed to overwhelm with my womanly charms, when he doesn't even show up?'

"He was in Assembly," said Gina. "I saw him. Here he is now."

In bounded Mr Billingham, with his mop-top and his long long legs. Just about every girl in 3F was, or had been, dreadfully in love with Mr Billingham, despite the knowledge of the existence of a Mrs Billingham, and two little Billinghams. His charm was endless, and his lessons such fun. "Oh, I'm bored with base eight!" he would cry, and, hurling the book to the floor, would proceed to write a series of weird symbols on the board - "and there's a prize for the first one to work out the next two in the series." Or sometimes he would write out a problem on the board, always with a catch; like the one where train A leaves London for Glasgow travelling at 60 mph and half an hour later train B leaves Glasgow for London travelling at 80 mph, which train is nearer to London when they meet? And, he would add mischievously, give the date of birth of both the drivers. Always there was a prize for the winner, generally a boiled sweet, though this caused problems; the most frequent winner was Mandy Lester, and she was diabetic and couldn't have sweets. So Mr Billingham would pick up a piece of chalk, or extract a wilting flower from the vase on the table, and present it to her with a bow. You couldn't help but enjoy Maths, however hopeless you might be at it. Katie was more hopeless than almost anybody, and it was her favourite lesson. There was one more point in Mr Billingham's favour, a very good point; he thought the prefects a terrific joke. "*Ja, mein Kommandant!*" he had been heard to murmur, after speaking to one. It was very endearing.

They worked quite hard for the first half hour. Then Mr Billingham got bored with right-angled triangles, seized the chalk and quickly drew a football league table with certain figures missing. "Deduce the missing numbers," he said, gleefully. "A super Electrolux washing machine for the winner."

"A flippin' humbug, you mean."

"Do I detect a note of disbelief in your dulcet tones? Come on now, Katie, surprise us all. Stun us. Look here. Team B drew all their matches. That's the big giveaway."

"Is it?" said Katie, blankly. Peter Farmer won in the end. Mandy Lester didn't finish it at all, but then, she was looking a bit seedy, today.

They had English next. Five minutes before the end of the lesson, Katie whispered: "D'you want to use the toilets, at break?"

"Yup."

"Me too. So let's run like mad and get there quick, 'cos there'll be an awful queue." Standing in queues was not suited to Katie's nature. As soon as the bell went, they charged.

"What if it's Cleo?"

"If it's Cleo," said Katie, "then we burst." But there, propped against the washbasins in a resigned sort of way, was Judy Lever. They liked Judy; they knew her from last year's school play, which they'd all been involved in.

"Dear dear," said Katie, shaking her head in sorrow. "Caught in the act. The phantom toilet roll fiend of Compton Park. I'm afraid

98

I'll have to report this, Judy, to the highest authority…"

"Cheeky monkey," said Judy, tweaking her ear. "Honestly. What a way to spend break. If I knew who was doing this I'd kick them from here to Thursday fortnight. Oh, by the way, d'you remember I asked you to ask round your form for people to help with scenery for this year's play? I don't suppose by any miracle you found someone?"

"Oh yes," said Gina. "Katie went round and told everyone how much time they'd get off lessons, if they helped. I've got a great list of people for you."

"Really? That's marvellous. I was getting quite desperate, I was. Come on, then, where is it?"

"In my formroom," said Gina.

"She gets me a list, and she leaves it in her formroom." Judy raised her eyes to heaven. "I could do with it today… Are you first or second dinner?"

"Second."

"Good - could you bring it to me at twelve fifteen, then? In the hall, say."

"Yeah, OK." People were beginning to arrive; they disappeared into the cubicles.

"Aw Judy," said Katie, all finished and

hands, lingeringly, washed. "You aren't really going to throw us out into the sub-arctic, are you?"

"'Fraid I've got to," said Judy. "Much as it goes against the grain, laying down the law all over the place. No option."

"Do you *like* being a prefect, Judy?"

"You're joking. Petty officialdom and silly rules and doing the staff's dirty work for them. And it eats huge great chunks out of your free time."

"Can't you say no?"

"Refuse to be a prefect? Now you're really joking. The world would end. And my prospects with it. Now, stop trying to distract me, when I'm supposed to be throwing you out."

"I'll have a nervous breakdown," said Katie, "like that First Year, Julia whatsit."

"That'll be the day. You've got nerves of cast iron. And there's a rule about Third Years having breakdowns. It's definitely forbidden."

"Especially in the corridors," said Gina.

"Out!" said Judy. They gave in. Well, they'd used up a nice lot of break. As they left another two prefects arrived to give Judy some rather belated support.

"Why are prefects like 98a buses?" asked

100

Katie, and answered it herself: "They go around in threes, and they're almost totally empty on top."

"Expect you never have to wait half an hour for one," said Gina. "They're always there."

"I wonder what gets into them, really." They were circling the Science Block again, stamping and shivering. "This power mania that seems to take over. I mean, they must remember what it was like when *they* were lower school and the prefects were beastly to *them*. You'd think they'd be more - enlightened."

"Yes, well it obviously doesn't work like that, does it? I suppose they get their revenge, only they get it on the wrong people. And the whole thing just goes on and on."

"Perpetuates itself," said Katie, who was good with words. "Well, I don't want to end up like that. I'm not having my beautiful character warped. That's a very good reason for leaving after the fifth year. Not that I wouldn't anyway."

"Um," said Gina; she knew full well that she herself would most certainly not be allowed to leave at sixteen. Her parents would go berserk if she even suggested it. She did wish Katie wasn't so determined to leave. They could have such fun in the sixth. They could be the first nice prefects in the history of the world. Well, apart from Judy. She mustn't forget that list.

Next lesson was History (Wars of the Roses) in their formroom with Miss Fleming; Gina got the list from her desk and put it in her satchel. Then off to Room 21 for Geography (glaciers). Only Mr Morgan wasn't there. After five minutes the usual 'Have you seen him today?' began; shortly afterwards in came a teacher, one of the new young ones, with a pile of green exercise books.

"Mr Morgan's not here," she said, "so I'm sitting with you. Just get on with something quietly." This made her position clear; she was saying, "you keep the noise down to a gentle buzz and let me get on with my marking and I don't care if you do Geography or the football pools." 3F nodded in approval. Katie got a book out, more for show than because she intended reading it. Gina considered, then pulled out her drawing pad. She was in a drawing mood.

Drawing was Gina's great talent. People often wondered what Katie, witty sharp comical Katie, saw in someone so quiet and unKatie-like as Gina. This was foolish. Every comic needs a straight man - or woman - and in any case Gina had a strong and quirky sense of humour of her own. She expressed it in her drawing, which mostly took the form of cartoons. She could draw anybody - cruel caricature, instantly recognizable. Katie would sigh with envy; to her, this was a good deal cleverer, and funnier, than anything she could do or say. The two of them set each other off perfectly, their friendship was rock solid.

"Do Cleo," Katie hissed now. Gina nodded. She had intended to do Cleo, lots of Cleos. She experimented first with a trio of double decker bus Cleos, travelling in convoy, but this was difficult, and would need to be worked on at length. She took a new sheet and drew Cleo and Stuart standing grimly before their front door, and a little row of freezing, imploring children, the youngest in a pram. "No! Outside!" she printed at the bottom. Then she did the same scene again, at night, Stuart in pyjamas, Cleo in curlers, children half buried in a snowdrift. Oh, this was fun, this was the life. Gina wanted more than anything to be a cartoonist. She couldn't imagine being happy doing anything else. But her parents wanted her to be a doctor. Trouble ahead. Gina tried not to think of it. She drew Cleo with sub-machine gun opening fire on a group of First Years; Cleo in SS uniform with swastika armband, standing in front of a mirror and trying on a Hitler moustache.

"Oh Gina, that's absolutely brill." The lesson was over, only now did Katie dare to look, in case she couldn't swallow down her laughter. "God, if they printed those in the school magazine! How much better than the Annual Report of the History Society. Keep them safe. We'll publish them one day. I'll write the words."

"I do keep them," said Gina, stuffing them into her bag. "I've kept them all. Oh heck - the list! I'll have to run." She tore off at breakneck speed. Katie followed at a more leisurely pace, depositing her bag in the formroom before strolling along to the hall. As she approached she saw Cleo Langham, clearly preparing for another stint of duty, warming up her vocal chords with a few gentle shrieks before moving on to the heavy stuff. Gina and Judy were leaning against one of the tables, apparently deep in conversation. Katie thought it prudent not to linger, not with Cleo on the rampage. She'd better wait outside. Where was all this snow then? You could never believe a word they said, those weather forecasters.

"Took your time," she grumbled, when Gina eventually emerged.

"Sorry. She went all through the list, wanted to know who'd be actually helpful and who'd just mess around." They began to pace up and down. A whole horrible half hour before they could go in to dinner, lovely warm dinner. The icy hard ground froze their feet; feet were the first to go, then hands and noses.

"And then I... oh hell's bells."

"What?"

"I left my satchel there, didn't I. On the table. And - oh my God, Cleo's on duty."

"So?"

"Well, she's not likely to leave it there, is she? A satchel in the hall? It wasn't like Katie to be so slow. "She'll pick it up, won't she, and have a look inside to see whose it is, and what's the first thing she'll see? The cartoons."

"Oh strewth." That, thought Gina, was putting it very mildly. "Look, don't panic."

"There's nothing else to do," said Gina, panicking.

"Yes there is. Just go in, right, and say you've left your satchel, by mistake, when you were talking to Judy - make a point of that, you were only there at all because a prefect sent for you - and she'll probably just say, get it and get out. No harm done. Look, Gina, you've got to. I can't go, I'm supposed to be avoiding her. You've got to. Think what'll happen if you don't."

Gina thought of it. She gulped, turned and went. She almost walked into Cleo. She repeated exactly what Katie had told her to say. "Too bad," said Cleo. "You'll just have to leave it here, won't you, and perhaps you won't be so careless another time. Any excuse to sneak indoors. I'll take charge of it. You can collect it from me before afternoon registration. Now buzz off. Nobody needs a satchel to eat their dinner. Get outside."

And that was that.

"She's only got to lift the flap," Gina said despairingly, "and it wasn't fastened, I know it wasn't, 'cos I'd just taken the list out of it."

"We have to get it," said Katie. "At once. Now, let's think. All legal entrances guarded by prefects. Windows unreachable. No chimneys to do the Santa Claus bit. So what's left?"

"We could dig a tunnel," said Gina, with sarcasm. There was no need for Katie to *enjoy* this. It wasn't her bag.

"Staff door," said Katie. "It's the only way. Don't look like that. It's the only door not guarded. And any of the staff who go home for dinner, or go out or anything, should have gone by now. It should be dead quiet."

"Should be." Gina didn't like it. The staff entrance, and all that side of the school, where they parked their cars, was out of bounds. And so many teachers using it. They would almost certainly be caught. And yet - it was ideally situated. The staff door led into a little lobby, which led in turn directly into the main hall. She imagined Cleo, looking at those cartoons. They had to try.

"Attagirl," said Katie. They made their way around the side of the building, pressing tightly against the wall until the point where the drive swung away to pass through a sort of shrubbery. Gina was shaking and queasy with nerves. It was so menacingly quiet here, and at any moment a car might charge round the corner - it might be Mrs Hooper's car…

"All clear," whispered Katie. And then she stopped. Stopped dead. And pointed dumbly. There was a body in the shrubbery.

It was a couple of feet back from the drive, between two bushy plants. Passing in a car you probably wouldn't even notice it. Katie stepped forward. "Oh Lord," she said. "It's Mandy."

"Mandy?" Gina rushed to her side; an anonymous body was quite a different thing from a body that was Mandy - though which was worse? "Oh, Katie, she isn't dead?"

"Course she's not dead," said Katie angrily; at first she had thought so, and that moment of helpless disbelieving numbing horror was not something she would easily forget. "She's in a coma, isn't she?" They all knew about the danger of comas for a diabetic, but they'd never seen Mandy in one before.

"But if she's not moved from here soon she will be. It's flippin' perishing. She'll get pneumonia..." Katie moved to lift Mandy, who was lying on her side. She'd hit her face when she fell; it was scratched and bleeding. Then she hesitated. She'd always thought you shouldn't move unconscious people - and she didn't really know a thing about diabetes, there might be something you had to do to someone in a coma before you moved them - they might kill her. "We'd better get Mrs Ross," she said. "Come on!" They ran, hell

108

for leather, round the final bend of the drive, up to the staff door and inside, through the lobby, flung open the door to the hall - and there, as if waiting for them, stood Cleo Langham.

"Now you've really done it. Persistent disobedience, and out of bounds. I'm reporting this to Mrs Hooper."

"Cleo, get out of the way, you stupid nurd, there's a girl out there in a coma..."

Cleo didn't budge. Her body blocked the entrance; she spread her legs to prevent a possible dash round the side, and to anchor herself more firmly. "Oh come on, you can do better than that. I've had one already pretending she was going to pass out. She was much more convincing than you. You could use her in the school play... what the hell d'you think you're doing?" Katie had already done it. She had dived through Cleo's legs and was even now rolling to her feet on the other side. "I don't believe it..."

"Run, Katie," shouted Gina, and pushed past Cleo into the hall. Katie was already at the staff room door; as she raised her hand to knock, it opened, and out came Mr Billingham - dear, wonderful Mr Billingham. He looked down enquiringly at Katie from the lofty heights of his six foot three.

"Mandy," said Katie. "She's lying in the shrubbery, in a coma."

"Right," said Mr Billingham, and disappeared back inside at speed. Seconds later, Mrs Ross (Games) appeared, Mr Billingham at her heels.

"These two," said Mr Billingham, indicating Katie and Gina.

"Come on," said Mrs Ross, "show me where she is. Hurry. Out of the *way*, Cleo." They all ran outside, Cleo following at a distance.

"Let's get her indoors," said Mrs Ross, checking for Mandy's pulse. Mrs Ross had gone quite pale. "Maureen's phoned for an ambulance. The poor child." She picked Mandy up with as much ease as if she were a kitten. Cleo sidled forward, her face registering something like alarm.

"Oh Cleo," said Katie. "This must be the girl who told you she was going to pass out, and you didn't believe her. How awful."

For a moment nobody said anything. Then Mrs Ross paused and asked: "Is this true, Cleo?"

"They try so many excuses," Cleo said faintly.

"How long ago?"

"Five - maybe ten minutes."

Mrs Ross just looked at her. A look that said more than words ever could. Then she marched off, carrying Mandy's inert body.

"Cleo," said Mr Billingham. "In future I think it would be as well if you were to temper your vigilance with a little common sense."

Cleo bit her lip, turned and walked back inside. The others followed. Back in the hall, Katie drew Gina aside, and pointed. "Your satchel, look. Go get it."

Gina looked quickly at Mandy, who had roused a little, muttered something and lapsed back into unconsciousness. Well, it wasn't going to make any difference to Mandy, was it, if she got her satchel out of Cleo's clutches. She picked it up and went off to dump it in the formroom.

Katie pulled at Mr Billingham's sleeve. "She is going to be all right, isn't she?"

"I hope so." He looked rather shaken himself. Mandy's face was almost waxen, now, under those cuts. Katie realized that the cuts probably weren't so bad as they looked.

"She'll be all right," said Mrs Ross. "If she was on her feet and talking to Cleo ten minutes ago, there shouldn't be any lasting damage. Where's that ambulance? I suppose she made her way around to the staff entrance thinking that was the only place she was likely to be taken seriously." She gave Cleo another look. Cleo moved away. "Ah, good, here they are now." She stepped forward to speak to the ambulance men. "I'll go with her," she said. "Has someone notified the parents?"

"Maureen said she'd ring them," said Mr Billingham. Katie wondered vaguely who Maureen might be. The ambulance men - one of them was a woman - lifted Mandy on to a stretcher-thing, and covered her with red blankets; the ambulance party moved off.

"Awful thing, diabetes," Mr Billingham said to Katie, and to Gina, who had just returned. "I suppose she's either not had her insulin for some reason, or had the insulin but not enough food to go with it. Either way, you go into a coma. Awful. Friend of my sister's has it. Now you two." He was sounding more loke his proper self. "For the life of me I can't imagine what you were doing in the shrubbery. But it's extremely fortunate that you were, isn't it?"

"Extremely," said Katie.

"So I think perhaps not too many questions will be asked... you did very well to act so promptly. Not panicking."

"I nearly panicked," said Gina. "She looked so..."

"Dead," said Katie, never one to mince words. She was thinking - couldn't help thinking - if Gina hadn't done the cartoons, if Judy hadn't asked for the list today, if Gina hadn't forgotten her bag, if Cleo had let her fetch it, then they wouldn't have been in the shrubbery, and Mandy would be... no. They'd never know. One of the staff might have driven past seconds later, and seen her. It was, Katie decided, more than likely. And, meanwhile, here was Cleo again, coming their way. To apologize perhaps?

"Mr Billingham?"

"Katie?"

"Seeing as we did so well and acting so promptly and didn't panic, and Mandy being one of your best pupils and all, would you do us a big favour? When Cleo gets here would you call me Sharon and Gina Lucy?"

Mr Billingham looked perplexed. "Certainly not, Sharon," he said as Cleo came to a halt behind them. "Out of the question, Lucy. And now I really must get back to my once piping hot tea and my Embassy Slim Panatella. If you care to come and see me after school I'll let you know what news we have from the hospital."

Exit Mr Billingham, inscrutably. Katie and Gina turned to face Cleo. Cleo glowered. Her face said all sorts of things. But her mouth produced one word only.

"Outside!"

THE HITCH-HIKER

BY ROALD DAHL

I had a new car. It was an exciting toy, a big BMW 3.3 Li, which means 3.3 litre, long wheelbase, fuel injection. It had a top speed of 129 mph and terrific acceleration. The body was pale blue. The seats inside were darker blue and they were made of leather, genuine soft leather of the finest quality. The windows were electrically operated and so was the sun-roof. The radio aerial popped up when I switched on the radio, and disappeared when I switched it off. The powerful engine growled and grunted impatiently at slow speeds, but at sixty miles an hour the growling stopped and the motor began to purr with pleasure.

I was driving up to London by myself. It was a lovely June day. They were haymaking in the fields and there were buttercups along both sides of the road. I was whispering along at seventy miles an hour, leaning back comfortably in my seat, with no more than a couple of fingers resting lightly on the wheel to keep her steady. Ahead of me I saw a man thumbing a lift. I touched the footbrake and brought the car to a stop beside him. I always stopped for hitch-hikers. I knew just how it used to feel to be standing on the side of a country road watching the cars go by. I hated drivers for pretending they didn't see me, especially the ones in big cars with three empty seats. The large expensive cars seldom stopped. It was always the smaller ones that offered you a lift, or the old rusty ones, or the ones that were already crammed full of children and the driver would say, "I think we can squeeze in one more."

The hitch-hiker poked his head through the open window and said, "Going to London, guv'nor?"

"Yes," I said. "Jump in."

He got in and I drove on.

He was a small ratty-faced man with grey teeth. His eyes were dark and quick and clever, like a rat's eyes, and his ears were slightly pointed at the top. He had a cloth cap on his head and he was wearing a greyish-coloured jacket with enormous pockets. The grey jacket, together with the quick eyes and the pointed ears, made him look more than anything like some sort of huge human rat.

"What part of London are you headed for?" I asked him.

"I'm goin' right through London and out the other side," he said. "I'm goin' to Epsom, for the races. It's Derby Day today."

"So it is," I said. "I wish I were going with you. I love betting on horses."

"I never bet on horses," he said. "I don't even watch 'em run. That's a stupid silly business."

"Then why do you go?" I asked.

He didn't seem to like that question. His little ratty face went absolutely blank and he sat there staring straight ahead at the road, saying nothing.

"I expect you help to work the betting machines or something like that," I said.

"That's even sillier," he answered. "There's no fun working them lousy machines and selling tickets to mugs. Any fool could do that."

There was a long silence. I decided not to question him any more. I remembered how irritated I used to get in my hitch-hiking days when drivers kept asking me questions. Where are you going? Why are you going there? What's your job? Are you married? Do you have a girl friend? What's her name? How old are you? And so on and so forth. I used to hate it.

"I'm sorry," I said. "It's none of my business what you do. The trouble is, I'm a writer, and most writers are terrible nosey parkers."

"You write books?" he asked.

"Yes."

"Writin' books is OK," he said. It's what I call a skilled trade. I'm in a skilled trade too. The folks I despise is them that spend all their lives doin' crummy old routine jobs with no skill in em' at all. You see what I mean?"

"Yes."

"The secret of life," he said, "is to become very very good at somethin' that's very very 'ard to do."

"Like you," I said.

"Exactly. You and me both."

"What makes you think that I'm any good at my job?" I asked. "There's an awful lot of bad writers around."

"You wouldn't be drivin' about in a car like this if you weren't no good at it," he answered. "It must've cost a tidy packet, this little job."

"It wasn't cheap."

"What can she do flat out?" he asked.

"One hundred and twenty-nine miles an hour," I told him.

"I'll bet she won't do it."

"I'll bet she will."

"All car makers is liars," he said. "You can buy any car you like and it'll never do what the makers say it will in the ads."

"This one will."

"Open 'er up then and prove it," he said. "Go on, guv'nor, open 'er right up and let's see what she'll do."

There is a roundabout at Chalfont St Peter and immediately beyond it there's a long straight section of dual carriageway. We came out of the roundabout on to the carriageway and I pressed my foot down on the accelerator. The big car leaped forward as though she'd been stung. In ten seconds or so, we were doing ninety.

"Lovely!" he cried. "Beautiful! Keep goin'!"

I had the accelerator jammed right down against the floor and I held it there.

"One hundred!" he shouted... "A hundred and five!... A hundred and ten! ... A hundred and fifteen! Go on! Don't slack off!"

I was in the outside lane and we flashed past several cars as though they were standing still - a green Mini, a big cream-coloured Citroen, a white Land-Rover, a huge truck with a container on the back, an orange-coloured Volkswagen Minibus...

"A hundred and twenty" my passenger shouted, jumping up and down. "Go on! Go on! Get 'er up to one-two-nine!"

At that moment, I heard the scream of a police siren. It was so loud it seemed to be right inside the car, and then a policeman on a motor-cycle loomed up alongside us on the inside lane and went past us and raised a hand for us to stop.

"Oh, my sainted aunt!" I said. "That's torn it!"

The policeman must have been doing about a hundred and thirty when he passed us, and he took plenty of time slowing down. Finally, he pulled into the side of the road and I pulled in behind him. "I didn't know police motorcycles could go as fast as that," I said rather lamely.

"That one can," my passenger said. "It's the same make as yours. It's a BMW R90S. Fastest bike on the road. That's what they're using nowadays."

The policeman got off his motor-cycle and leaned the machine sideways on to its prop stand. Then he took of his gloves and placed them carefully on the seat. He was in no hurry now. He had us where he wanted us and he knew it.

"This is real trouble," I said. "I don't like it one bit."

"Don't talk to 'im any more than is necessary, you understand," my companion said. "Just sit tight and keep mum."

Like an executioner approaching his victim, the policeman came strolling slowly towards us. He was a big meaty man with a belly, and his blue breeches were skintight around his enormous thighs. His goggles were pulled up on to the helmet, showing a smouldering red face with wide cheeks.

We sat there like guilty schoolboys, waiting for him to arrive.

"Watch out for this man," my passenger whispered. "He looks mean as the devil."

The policeman came round to my open window and placed one meaty hand on the sill. "What's the hurry?" he said.

"No hurry, officer," I answered.

"Perhaps there's a woman in the back having a baby and you're rushing her to hospital? Is that it?"

"No, officer."

"Or perhaps your house is on fire and you're dashing home to rescue the family from upstairs?" His voice was dangerously soft and mocking.

"My house isn't on fire, officer."

"In that case," he said, "you've got yourself into a nasty mess, haven't you? Do you know what the speed limit is in this country?"

"Seventy," I said.

"And do you mind telling me exactly what speed you were doing just now?"

I shrugged and didn't say anything.

When he spoke next, he raised his voice so loud that I jumped. "*One hundred and twenty miles per hour!*" he barked. "That's *fifty* miles an hour over the limit!"

He turned his head and spat out a big gob of spit. It landed on the wing of my car and started sliding down over my beautiful blue paint. Then he turned back again and stared hard at my passenger. "And who are you?" he asked sharply.

"He's a hitch-hiker," I said. "I'm giving him a lift."

"I didn't ask you," he said. "I asked him."

"'Ave I done somethin' wrong?" my passenger asked. His voice was as soft and oily as haircream.

"That's more than likely," the policeman answered. "Anyway, you're a witness. I'll deal with you in a minute. Driving licence," he snapped, holding out his hand.

I gave him my driving licence.

He unbuttoned the left-hand breast-pocket of his tunic and brought out the dreaded book of tickets. Carefully, he copied the name and address from my licence. Then he gave it back to me. He strolled round to the front of the car and read the number from the number-plate and wrote that down as well. He filled in the date, the time and the details of my offence. Then he tore out the top copy of the ticket. But before handing it to me, he checked that all the information had come through clearly on his own carbon copy. Finally, he replaced the book in his tunic pocket and fastened the button.

"Now you," he said to my passenger, and he walked around to the other side of the car. From the other breast-pocket he produced a small black notebook. "Name?" he snapped.

"Michael Fish," my passenger said.

"Address?"

"Fourteen, Windsor Lane, Luton."

"Show me something to prove this is your real name and address," the policeman said.

My passenger fished in his pockets and came out with a driving licence of his own. The policeman checked the name and address and handed it back to him. "What's your job?" he asked sharply.

"I'm an 'od carrier."

"A what?"

"An 'od carrier."

"Spell it."

"H-O-D C-A-..."

"That'll do. And what's a hod carrier, may I ask?"

"An 'od carrier, officer, is a person 'oo carries the cement up the ladder to the bricklayer. And the 'od is what 'ee carries it in. It's got a long 'andle, and on the top you've got two bits of wood set at an angle..."

"All right, all right. Who's your employer?"

"Don't 'ave one. I'm unemployed."

The policeman wrote all this down in the black notebook. Then he returned the book to its pocket and did up the button.

"When I get back to the station I'm going to do a little checking up on you," he said to my passenger.

"Me? What've I done wrong?" the rat-faced man asked.

"I don't like your face, that's all," the policeman said. "And we just might have a picture of it somewhere in our files." He strolled round the car and returned to my window.

"I suppose you know you're in serious trouble," he said to me.

"Yes, officer."

"You won't be driving this fancy car of yours again for a very long time, not after we've finished with you. You won't be driving any car again come to that for several years. And a good thing too. I hope they lock you up for a spell into the bargain."

"You mean prison?" I asked, alarmed.

"Absolutely," he said, smacking his lips. "In the clink. Behind the bars. Along with all the other criminals who break the law. And a hefty fine into the bargain. Nobody will be more pleased about that than me. I'll see you in court, both of you. You'll be getting a summons to appear."

He turned away and walked over to his motor-cycle. He flipped the prop stand back into position with his foot and swung his leg over the saddle. Then he kicked the starter and roared off up the road out of sight.

"Phew!" I gasped. "That's done it."

"We was caught," my passenger said. "We was caught good and proper."

"I was caught, you mean."

"That's right," he said. "What you goin' to do now, guv'nor?"

"I'm going straight up to London to talk to my solicitor," I said. I started the car and drove on.

"You mustn't believe what 'ee said to you about goin' to prison," my passenger said. "They don't put nobody in the clink just for speedin'."

"Are you sure of that?" I asked.

"I'm positive," he answered. "They can take your licence away and they can give you a whoppin' big fine, but that'll be the end of it."

I felt tremendously relieved.

"By the way," I said, "why did you lie to him?"

"Who, me?" he said. "What makes you think I lied?"

"You told me you were in a highly skilled trade."

"So I am," he said. "But it don't pay to tell everythin' to a copper."

"So what do you do?" I asked him.

"Ah," he said slyly. "That'd be tellin', wouldn't it?"

"Is it something you're ashamed of?"

"Ashamed?" he cried. "Me, ashamed of my job? I'm about as proud of it as anybody could be in the entire world!"

"Then why won't you tell me?"

"You writers really is nosey parkers, aren't you?" he said. "And you ain't goin' to be 'appy, I don't think, until you've found out exactly what the answer is?"

"I don't really care one way or the other," I told him, lying.

He gave me a crafty little ratty look out of the sides of his eyes. "I think you do care," he said. I can see it on your face that you think I'm some kind of a very peculiar trade and you're just achin' to know what it is."

I didn't like the way he read my thoughts. I kept quiet and stared at the road ahead.

"You'd be right, too," he went on. "I *am* in

a very peculiar trade. I'm in the queerest peculiar trade of 'em all."

I waited for him to go on.

"That's why I 'as to be extra careful 'oo I'm talkin' to, you see. 'Ow am I to know, for instance, you're not another copper in plain clothes?"

"Do I look like a copper?"

"No," he said. "You don't. And you ain't. Any fool could tell that."

He took from his pocket a tin of tobacco and a packet of cigarette papers and started to roll a cigarette. I was watching him out of one eye, and the speed with which he performed this rather difficult operation was incredible. The cigarette was rolled and ready in about five seconds. He ran his tongue along the edge of the paper, stuck it down and popped the cigarette between his lips. Then, as if from nowhere, a lighter appeared in his hand. The lighter flamed. The cigarette was lit. The lighter disappeared. It was altogether a remarkable performance.

"I've never seen anyone roll a cigarette as fast as that," I said.

"Ah," he said, taking a deep suck of smoke. "So you noticed."

"Of course I noticed. It was quite fantastic."

He sat back and smiled. It pleased him very much that I had noticed how quickly he could roll a cigarette. "You want to know what makes me able to do it?" he asked.

"Go on then."

"It's because I've got fantastic fingers. These fingers of mine," he said, holding up both hands high in front of him, "are quicker and cleverer than the fingers of the best piano player in the world!"

"Are you a piano player?"

"Don't be daft," he said. "Do I look like a piano player?"

I glanced at his fingers. They were so beautifully shaped, so slim and long and elegant, they didn't seem to belong to the rest of him at all. They looked more like the fingers of a brain surgeon or a watchmaker.

"My job," he went on, "is a hundred times more difficult than playin' the piano. Any twerp can learn to do that. There's titchy little kids learnin' to play the piano in almost any 'ouse you go into these days. That's right, ain't it?"

"More or less," I said.

"Of course it's right. But there's not one person in ten million can learn to do what I do. Not one in ten million! 'Ow about that?"

"Amazing," I said.

"You're darn right it's amazin'," he said.

"I think I know what you do," I said. "You do conjuring tricks. You're a conjurer."

"Me?" he snorted. "A conjurer? Can you picture me goin' round crummy kids' parties makin' rabbits come out of top 'ats?"

"Then you're a card player. You get people into card games and deal yourself marvelllous hands."

"Me! A rotten card-sharper!" he cried. "That's a miserable racket if ever there was one."

"All right. I give up."

I was taking the car slowly now, at no more than forty miles an hour, to make quite sure I wasn't stopped again. We had come on to the main London-Oxford road and were running down the hill towards Denham.

Suddenly my passenger was holding up a black leather belt in his hand. "Ever seen this before?" he asked. The belt had a brass buckle of unusual design.

"Hey!" I said. "That's mine, isn't it? It *is* mine! Where did you get it?"

He grinned and waved the belt gently from side to side. "Where d'you think I got it?" he said. "Off the top of your trousers, of course."

I reached down and felt for my belt. It was gone.

"You mean you took it off me while we've been driving along?" I asked, flabbergasted.

He nodded, watching me all the time with those little black ratty eyes.

"That's impossible," I said. "You'd have had to undo the buckle and slide the whole thing out through the loops all the way round. I'd have seen you doing it. And even if I hadn't seen you, I'd have felt it."

"Ah, but you didn't did you?" he said, triumphant. He dropped the belt on his lap, and now all at once there was a brown shoelace dangling from his finger. "And what about this, then?" he exclaimed, waving the shoelace.

"What about it?" I said.

"Anyone around 'ere missin' a shoelace?" he asked, grinning.

I glanced down at my shoes. The lace of one of them was missing. "Good grief!" I said. "How did you do that? I never saw you bending down."

"You never saw nothin'," he said proudly. "You never even saw me move an inch. And you know why?"

"Yes," I said. "Because you've got fantastic fingers."

"Exactly right!" he cried. "You catch on pretty quick, don't you?" He sat back and sucked away at his home-made cigarette, blowing the smoke out in a thin stream against the windshield. He knew he had impressed me greatly with those two tricks and this made him very happy. "I don't want to be late," he said. "What time is it?"

"There's a clock in front of you," I told him.

"I don't trust car clocks," he said. "What does your watch say?"

I hitched up my sleeve to look at the watch on my wrist. It wasn't there. I looked at the man. He looked back at me, grinning.

"You've taken that, too," I said.

He held out his hand and there was my watch lying in his palm. "Nice bit of stuff, this," he said. "Superior quality. Eighteen-carat gold. Easy to flog, too. It's never any trouble gettin' rid of quality goods."

"I'd like it back, if you don't mind," I said rather huffily.

He placed the watch carefully on the leather tray in front of him. "I wouldn't nick anythin' from you, guvnor," he said. "You're

133

my pal. You're giving me a lift."

"I'm glad to hear it," I said.

"All I'm doin' is answerin' your questions," he went on. "You asked me what I did for a livin' and I'm showin' you."

"What else have you got of mine?"

He smiled again, and now he started to take from the pocket of his jacket one thing after another that belonged to me - my driving licence, a key ring with four keys on it, some pound notes, a few coins, a letter from my publishers, my diary, a stubby old pencil, a cigarette lighter, and last of all, a beautiful old sapphire ring with pearls around it belonging to my wife. I was taking the ring up to the jeweller in London because one of the pearls was missing.

"Now there's another lovely piece of goods," he said, turning the ring over in his fingers. "That's eighteenth century, if I'm not mistaken, from the reign of King George the Third."

"You're right," I said, impressed. "You're absolutely right."

He put the ring on the leather tray with the other items.

"So you're a pickpocket," I said.

"I don't like that word," he answered. "It's a

coarse and vulgar word. Pickpockets is coarse and vulgar people who only do easy little amateur jobs. They lift money from blind old ladies."

"What do you call yourself, then?"

"Me? I'm a fingersmith. I'm a professional fingersmith." He spoke the words solemnly and proudly, as though he were telling me he was the President of the College of Surgeons or the Archbishop of Canterbury.

"I've never heard that word before," I said. "Did you invent it?"

"Of course I didn't invent it," he replied. "It's the name given to them who's risen to the very top of the profession. You've 'eard of a goldsmith and a silversmith, for instance. They're experts with gold and silver. I'm an expert with my fingers, so I'm a fingersmith."

"It must be an interesting job."

"It's a marvellous job," he answered. "It's lovely."

"And that's why you go to the races?"

"Race meetings is easy meat," he said. "You just stand around after the race, watchin' for the lucky ones to queue up and draw their money. And when you see someone collectin' a big bundle of notes, you simply follows after 'im and 'elps yourself. But don't get me wrong guv'nor. I never takes nothin' from a loser. Nor from poor people either. I only go after them as can afford it, the winners and the rich."

"That's very thoughtful of you," I said. "How often do you get caught?"

"Caught?" he cried, disgusted. "Me get caught! It's only pickpockets get caught. Fingersmiths never. Listen, I could take the false teeth out of your mouth if I wanted to and you wouldn't even catch me!"

"I don't have false teeth," I said.

"I know you don't," he answered. "Otherwise I'd 'ave 'ad 'em out long ago!"

I believed him. Those long slim fingers of his seemed able to do anything.

We drove on for a while without talking.

"That policeman's going to check up on you pretty thoroughly," I said. "Doesn't that worry you a bit?"

"Nobody's checkin' up on me," he said.

"Of course they are. He's got your name and address written down most carefully in his black book."

The man gave me another of his sly, ratty little smiles. "Ah," he said. "So 'ee 'as. But I'll bet 'ee ain't got it all written down in 'is memory as well. I've never known a copper yet with a decent memory. Some of 'em can't even remember their own names."

"What's memory got to do with it?" I asked. "It's written down in his book, isn't it?"

"Yes, guv'nor, it is. But the trouble is, 'ee's lost the book. "'Ee's lost both books, the one with my name in it and the one with yours."

In the long delicate fingers of his right hand, the man was holding up in triumph the two books he had taken from the policeman's pockets. "Easiest job I ever done," he announced proudly.

I nearly swerved the car into a milk-truck, I was so excited.

"That copper's got nothin' on either of us now," he said.

"You're a genius!" I cried.

"'Ee's got no names, no addresses, no car number, no nothin'," he said.

"You're brilliant!"

"I think you'd better pull off this main road as soon as possible," he said. "Then we'd better build a little bonfire and burn these books."

"You're a fantastic fellow," I exclaimed.

"Thank you guv'nor," he said. "It's always nice to be appreciated."

AFTER YOU, MY DEAR ALPHONSE

BY SHIRLEY JACKSON

Mrs Wilson was just taking the gingerbread out of the oven when she heard Johnny outside talking to someone. "Johnny," she called, "you're late. Come in and get your lunch."

"Just a minute, Mother," Johnny said. "After you, my dear Alphonse."

"After *you*, my dear Alphonse," another voice said.

"No, after *you*, my dear Alphonse," Johnny said.

Mrs Wilson opened the door. "Johnny," she said, "you come in this minute and get your lunch. You can play after you've eaten."

Johnny came in after her, slowly. "Mother," he said, "I brought Boyd home for lunch with me."

"Boyd?" Mrs Wilson thought for a moment. "I don't believe I've met Boyd. Bring him in, dear, since you've invited him. Lunch is ready."

"Boyd!" Johnny yelled. "Hey, Boyd, come on in!"

"I'm coming. Just got to unload this stuff."

"Well, hurry, or my mother'll be sore."

"Johnny, that's not very polite to either your friend or your mother," Mrs Wilson said. "Come sit down, Boyd."

As she turned to show Boyd where to sit, she saw he was a Negro boy, smaller than Johnny but about the same age. His arms were loaded with split kindling wood. "Where'll I put this stuff, Johnny?" he asked.

Mrs Wilson turned to Johnny. "Johnny," she said, "what did you make Boyd do? What is that wood?"

"Dead Japanese," Johnny said mildly. "We stand them in the ground and run over them with tanks."

"How do you do, Mrs Wilson?" Boyd said.

"How do you do, Boyd? You shouldn't let Johnny make you carry all that wood. Sit down now and eat lunch, both of you.

"Why shouldn't he carry the wood, Mother? It's his wood. We got it at his place."

"Johnny," Mrs Wilson, said, "go on and eat your lunch."

"Sure," Johnny said. He held out the dish of scarmbled eggs to Boyd. "After you, my dear Alphonse."

"After you, my dear Alphonse," Boyd said.

"After you, my dear Alphonse," Johnny said. They began to giggle.

"Are you hungry, Boyd?" Mrs Wilson said.

"Yes, Mrs Wilson."

"Well, don't you let Johnny stop you. He always fusses about eating, so you just see that you get a good lunch. There's plenty of food here for you to have all you want."

"Thank you, Mrs Wilson."

"Come on, Alphonse," Johnny said. He pushed half the scrambled eggs on to Boyd's plate. Boyd watched while Mrs Wilson put a dish of stewed tomatoes beside his plate.

"Boyd don't eat tomatoes, do you, Boyd?" Johnny said.

"*Doesn't* eat tomatoes, Johnny. And just

because you don't like them, don't say that about Boyd. Boyd will eat anything."

"Bet he won't," Johnny said, attacking his scrambled legs.

"Boyd wants to grow up and be a big strong man so he can work hard," Mrs Wilson. "I'll bet Boyd's father eats stewed tomatoes."

"My father eats anything he wants to," Boyd said.

"So does mine," Johnny said. "Sometimes he doesn't eat hardly anything. He's a little guy, though. Wouldn't hurt a flea."

"Mine's a little guy too," Boyd said.

"I'll bet he's strong, though," Mrs Wilson said. She hesitated. "Does he... work?"

"Sure," Johnny said. "Boyd's father works in a factory."

"There, you see?" Mrs Wilson said. "And he certainly has to be strong to do that - all that lifting and carrying at a factory."

"Boyd's father doesn't have to," Johnny said. "He's a foreman."

Mrs Wilson felt defeated. "What does your mother do, Boyd?"

"My mother?" Boyd was surprised. "She takes care of us kids."

"Oh. She doesn't work, then?"

"Why should she?" Johnny said through a

141

mouthful of eggs. "You don't work."

"You really don't want any stewed tomatoes, Boyd?"

"No, thank you, Mrs Wilson," Boyd said.

"No thank you. Mrs Wilson, no, thank you, Mrs Wilson, no, thank you, Mrs Wilson," Johnny said. "Boyd's sister's going to work though. She's going to be a teacher."

"That's a very fine attitude for her to have, Boyd." Mrs Wilson restrained an impulse to pat Boyd on the head. "I imagine you're all very proud of her?"

"I guess so," Boyd said.

"What about all your other brothers and sisters? I guess all of you want to make just as much of yourselves as you can."

"There's only me and Jean," Boyd said. "I don't know yet what I want to be when I grow up."

"We're going to be tank drivers, Boyd and me," Johnny said.

"Zoom." Mrs Wilson caught Boyd's glass of milk as Johnny's napkin ring, suddenly transformed into a tank, ploughed heavily across the table.

"Look Johnny," Boyd said. "Here's a foxhole. I'm shooting at you."

Mrs Wilson, with the speed born of long

experience, took the gingerbread off the shelf and placed it carefully between the tank and the foxhole.

"Now eat as much as you want to, Boyd," she said. "I want to see you get filled up."

"Boyd eats a little, but not as much as I do," Johnny said. "I'm bigger than he is."

"You're not much bigger," Boyd said. "I can beat you running."

Mrs Wilson took a deep breath. "Boyd," she said. Both boys turned to her. "Boyd, Johnny has some suits that are little too small for him, and a winter coat. It's not new, of course, but there's lots of wear in it still. And I have a few dresses that your mother or sister could probably use. Your mother can make them over into lots of things for all of you, and I'd be happy to give them to you. Suppose before you leave I make up a big bundle and then you and Johnny can take it over to your mother right away..." Her voice trailed off as she saw Boyd's puzzled expression.

"But I have plenty of clothes, thank you," he said. "And I don't think my mother knows how to sew very well, and anyway I guess we buy about everything we need. Thank you very much though.

"We don't have time to carry that old stuff

around, Mother," Johnny said. "We got to play tanks with the kids today."

Mrs Wilson lifted the plate of gingerbread off the table as Boyd was about to take another piece. "There are many little boys like you, Boyd, who would be very grateful for the clothes someone was kind enough to give them."

"Boyd will take them if you want him to, Mother," Johnny said.

"I didn't mean to make you mad, Mrs Wilson," Boyd said.

"Don't think I'm angry, Boyd, I'm just disappointed in you, that's all. Now let's not say anything more about it."

She began clearing the plates off the table, and Johnny took Boyd's hand and pulled him to the door. "'Bye, Mother," Johnny said. Boyd stood for a minute, staring at Mrs Wilson's back.

"After you, my dear Alphonse," Johnny said, holding the door open.

"Is your mother still mad?" Mrs Wilson heard Boyd ask in a low voice.

"I don't know," Johnny said. "She's screwy sometimes."

"So's mine," Boyd said. He hesitated. "After you, my dear Alphonse."

THINGY

BY CHRIS POWLING

Once upon a time there wasn't a Thingy - not really. Thingy was what you called someone whose name you couldn't remember. You'd say something like "Hey... er, Thingy... bring over the pencil-sharpner, would you?" Or some kid would say to you "Here, guess who we saw in the park last Saturday. Old... um... Thingy - you know who I mean." Somehow you did know, usually.

But then the name Thingy got attached to just one person - to Lorna Penfold. Lorna Penfold became the one and only Thingy.

After that if you called anyone else Thingy they bashed you up. If they were big enough, that is. If they weren't then they'd scowl and say 'yuk' and they'd pretend to brush something messy off their sleeve. No one wanted to be called the same name as Lorna Penfold.

Even the boys talked about her.

"Heard the latest?" someone would say.

"What about?"

"Thingy."

"No. What's up?"

"Well - it's about her dad, really. Old man Penfold. He's in prison again. Got taken away last week."

"What for?"

"Don't know. But it's definitely true. My mum knows someone who knows the welfare-worker. Says they're having to clean the house from top to bottom."

"Why?"

"Dog's muck."

"Dog's muck?"

"Dog's muck. From his greyhounds. They had the run of the house, they reckon. Never got let out. All the assistance money went on feeding them. Thingy's dad'll go mad when he gets back."

Some of the gossip about Thingy you could only whisper, though. About her mum, for example. And another subject nobody liked to discuss out loud was how Thingy came to have only one-and-a-half arms instead of two.

This was the first thing other kids noticed. Her tattered clothes and her smelliness only came later. Just about where her elbow should have been, Thingy's right arm ended in a flap of skin like a balloon not fully blown up. Everyone hated the sight of it. It was strange when, for a while, Thingy's stump made her the most important person in the playground.

This happened in the Spring term. The air was still sharp but there were smudges of green in the churchyard trees next door and it was the time for gangs. Every kid had to be in a gang. And to get in a gang you had to do the membership tests set by the gang-leader. You had to run fast enough or jump high enough or do something daring. All the time you saw the kids being tested.

Only one gang-leader so far had refused to name the test for his gang. He was the biggest, most important leader of all - Raymond Essex. After four days the other big and important boys were tired of being kept waiting.

"Hey, Raymond," Teddy said. "Is it today?"

"Might be."

"Come on, Raymond," said Pete. "All the other gangs are already formed, practically."

"Maybe we should join one of them," said Kit bitterly. "Or start one of our own."

"Go ahead," said Raymond.

That shut Kit up. Aloofly, Raymond scanned the playground. On the fringe of a group of smaller boys was Thingy. She always preferred the boys to leave her out than the girls.

"Hey, Thingy!" shouted Raymond.

Thingy turned. When she saw who was calling, her mouth gaped open in surprise.

"Come over here!" Raymond beckoned.

The big and most important boys looked at each other pulling faces. Thingy trotted over.

"Want to help with the tests for my gang, Thingy?" Raymond asked.

"What?"

"You don't have to," said Raymond.

"Yes I will," blurted Thingy.

"You sure?"

Thingy nodded warily.

"Right," said Raymond. "All-y, all-y in those who want to be in my gang."

"All-y, all-y in!" whooped the others.

Even kids who already belonged to gangs, or who knew they wouldn't stand a chance, gathered round. Raymond's tests were always worth watching.

"Okay," said Raymond. "There's only one thing you've got to do if you want to get in my gang. Who wants to try it?"

A circle of hands shot up. He glanced at Thingy again.

"Sure you want to help?" he asked.

"Course," said Thingy.

The corner of Raymond's mouth twitched.

"Here we go, then - the membership test for my gang. All you've got to do is this. See Thingy's stump?"

Everyone looked. Thingy lifted it uncertainly.

"You've got to kiss it," said Raymond.

Several kids gasped. All round, the raised hands wilted. Some dropped altogether. Thingy's face was stiff as a mask. Beneath her lank hair her eyes glinted. No one spoke. Raymond's grin was half a sneer and half a giggle.

"Nobody fancy it?" he asked. "Well that's that, then. Sorry, Thingy. They don't seem to want to kiss your stump. I'll just have to think up some easier test for next week -

maybe. All-y, all-y out, then."

"Just a minute," Teddy said.

Those who'd already begun to move off, stopped. Something about Teddy's voice held them.

"You got something to say?" Raymond asked.

"Sure," said Teddy. "You serious that's the test for your gang?"

"Just said it, didn't I?"

"And you're not going to back down on it?"

"Me?" said Raymond. "I'm not doing any backing down. Thought you lot had done that."

"No we haven't," said Teddy. "Just couldn't believe it was so simple to get in your gang, that's all."

He stepped forward.

"Okay, Thingy?"

Quickly he bent and kissed her stump. When he straightened his face was expressionless.

"There," he shrugged. "Really tough that was. Anyone else want to join Raymond's gang?"

There was a pause while the kids looked at each other.

"I will," said Pete.

"I will," Kit echoed.

Most of the bigger and more important boys called out then. They edged forward one after the other. Some of them made a face when it came to their turn or rubbed their mouth afterwards in a funny way. Others treated it like Teddy. Soon all the kids you'd expect to be in Raymond's gang had joined.

"That's the lot," snapped Raymond. "No more. All-y, all-y out."

"Wait a minute," Jimmy protested. "I'm next in line. I want to take the test."

Raymond scowled and shook his head.

"No little kids. You're only eight."

"What's the matter? It's if you can do the test - that's what counts. Isn't that right, Teddy?"

"That's right," said Teddy.

"If we let him join they'll all join," Raymond snorted. "We won't be a gang, we'll be a bunch of - of babysitters!"

"Can't help that," Teddy said. "You set the test. Told you it was too simple. Mind you, there is one way you could keep the shrimps out without backing down."

"How's that?"

"Well... *you* can't stop people taking the

151

test. That's not fair. But Thingy could. All she's got to do is not to let anyone else kiss her stump. And you could make sure of that quite easily."

"How?"

"Let Thingy join the gang. She wouldn't muck up her own gang, would she?"

"What!" Raymond yelped.

"How can you stop her?" Teddy pointed out. "She's only got to kiss her own stump and she's joined. Want to be in the gang, Thingy?"

Thingy's fixed look had slipped. She couldn't believe it.

"Yes," she said.

"Well, kiss your stump then and you're in."

Still staring at Teddy, Thingy brushed her arm with her lips. In the crowd someone sniggered.

"That," Raymond grated, "just about puts the tin lid on it."

"No it doesn't," said Teddy. "What about you?"

"Me?"

"Your turn. You haven't done the test yourself yet."

"*Me*?"

"You," Teddy insisted.

Raymond swallowed. "I don't get it. What's the matter with you? What you sticking up for her for? You in love with her or something? Hey, get this you lot! Teddy Beckenham's got a crush on Thingy! When you going to marry him, Thingy?"

"When're you going to take the test?" asked Teddy, coolly. "Or are you scared to kiss Thingy's stump?" Standing on either side of him, Kit and Pete felt Teddy trembling. You'd never guess this from the way he looked, though. Next to Godfrey Fanshaw he always had been the best actor in the school.

"I'm not scared," said Raymond. "But I'm not going to take the test either."

"You've got to," shrugged Teddy. "Gangleader's got to show he can do his own test."

"Not this one," said Raymond.

"You can't be leader, then. Come to that you can't even be in the gang."

"That so? Mind telling me who *is* leader of the gang, then? You, maybe?"

"I was first," Teddy said. "Reckon I must be."

"Reckon you must be," repeated Raymond. "Reckon you're a good enough fighter to be leader of the gang?"

"Don't know."

"Reckon you'd like to find out? After school say?" Teddy's chin trembled.

"Okay," he said.

"That ain't fair - that ain't fair!" Thingy burst out. "You can murder him!"

"Your girlfriend thinks it's not fair," said Raymond. "Do you think it's fair?"

"Course," said Teddy. "She's not my girlfried," he added.

"No? Funny - thought she was. After school, then. And no chanting."

"No chanting," Teddy agreed.

"That ain't fair!" Thingy screamed. "That ain't fair!"

In a way she was right. Without chanting Teddy hadn't a hope. When the kids yelled "Fight! Fight! Fight!" a teacher came running. It was a way of making sure no one got badly hurt. With silent watches, though, it could easily be ten minutes before a grown-up realized what was happening. It was a point of honour that the fight went on till then. And ten minutes was more than enough for Raymond. He was the most vicious fighter in the district.

All afternoon Teddy had to put up with kids who smiled wryly and asked him what flowers he wanted. Worse, he had to put up with Thingy who didn't take her eyes off him.

By five past four the playground was ready. Using the netball-markings, the kids had formed an arena. Those in the front had linked hands. In the centre were Raymond and Teddy. The silence was eerie. A few of the younger kids had started by calling "all-y, all-y in" but they were soon shut up. There was to be no chanting. Teddy had agreed to it.

"Okay?" asked Raymond.

"Okay."

Both boys edged apart a pace or two. They bunched their fists and dropped into a half-crouch. Somewhere at the back Thingy gave a howl of misery.

"That your girlfriend?" Raymond enquired.

Teddy swung with everything he'd got. The punch caught Raymond square on the chin. He staggered and nearly fell. Then he straightened up.

"That the best you can do?" he asked.

"'Fraid so," said Teddy.

"Well here's my second-best," said Raymond.

He lashed out. Teddy's head seemed to jerk almost fom his neck. Five or six more blows followed until Teddy crumbled. Sucking a tooth, Raymond waited for him to get up.

One of Teddy's eyes was already closed and blood smeared his nose and mouth. He got to his feet slowly. At once everyone gasped. Through thick lips Teddy was whistling - actually whistling. Casually he tossed the hair from his eyes. With dainty flicks he dusted himself down.

"Okay, fatso," he said. "You're knuckles have had it. My face is going to smash them to pieces."

"I see - a funny man," Raymond snarled.

Again he let fly, both fists thudding home. There was no way Teddy could dodge. His attempts to hit back were brushed aside. Down he went again. Some kids had turned away, unable to bear it. It was some while before Teddy got up this time. When he did... he blew Raymond a kiss. Raymond stared in disbelief. The he kicked savagely, catching Teddy on the shin. Teddy gasped.

"Naughty, naughty!" he said. "Lickle Donkey!"

Suddenly everyone could see what Teddy was trying to do. The more he was cut to pieces the more he was going to clown. "You won't be making a joke of it for long," Raymond spat.

He didn't sound convinced, though.

Already it might be too late. People had actually started laughing. Laughing! What if Teddy were carried off on a stretcher, still cocky? What if the littlest kids in the school were to copy Teddy's tactics? Uneasily Raymond lifted his fists. Teddy was jabbing the air with his like an old-time prize-fighter. He gave his opponent a huge wink. Raymond moved forward. But now, in a strange way, he looked as if he were going backwards.

Suddenly, a voice had the playground stockstill.

"You two boys stop that! This very second!"

It was old Miss Manly. She stood in the school doorway next to Thingy. No one had seen Thingy slip away.

"Thank you, Lorna," Miss Manly said. "You've been very sensible. You two boys come to my room. The rest of you get off home - this instant!"

Miss Manly stalked into school. She never had to wait to see if she was obeyed. The first kids were already moving towards the gate. As they passed Thingy they hissed under their breath and bared their teeth and made clawing movements with their hands.

"Very sensible, your girlfriend," Raymond remarked.

At the door Thingy tried to explain.

"You'd a got murdered," she said.

Teddy's swollen face was twisted with anger. He could hardly get the words out.

"You idiot! You stupid, stupid stinking idiot!"

The door slammed behind him. Thingy blinked. For a while she stood there staring at the woodwork. Then she turned for the other gate, into the churchyard. It was the long way round but she knew that if you ran and were lucky you could get home without meeting any big and important kids. If you were lucky you could get home without meeting any kids at all.

BLACK EYES

BY PHILIPPA PEARCE

Cousin Lucinda was coming to stay with Jane, just for the weekend.

Jane had never met Lucinda, but Jane's mother said she was a year younger than Jane, and they must all be very kind to her. Jane imagined the rest. She imagined a shy little girl with blue eyes and golden curls that bobbed about a round, rosy face. She would be rather cuddly, and they would play with their teddy-bears together.

But Lucinda was not at all like that. She was thin, and her hair was black without any curl to it, and her eyes were black in a white face - eyes as black as the Pontefract cakes you find in a liquorice assortment. Jane didn't like liquorice.

And Lucinda's teddy-bear had black eyes, too.

"He was exactly like your teddy-bear, to begin with," said Lucinda, "with eyes exactly like yours. But then one day my teddy-bear saw something horrid - so horrible - that his eyes dropped out. Then my mother made black eyes for him, with black wool." She paused for a quick breath. "But his eyes aren't made of ordinary black wool, and they're not stitched in an ordinary way. The black wool is magic, and my mother is a witch."

Jane said feebly, "My mother says your mother is her sister, so she can't be a witch."

"That's what your mother would like to believe," said Lucinda.

The two little girls were in their nightdresses, in Jane's room, that Lucinda was sharing for two nights. They had been playing and talking before going to bed.

Jane's father came in to say goodnight. He caught sight of the two teddies lying side by side. Lucinda's teddy never wore any clothes, she said; and Jane had just undressed her teddy for the night, taking off the trousers and jersey and balaclava helmet, with holes for the ears, that her mother had once knitted for him. So the two teddies lay side by side, with nothing on, and Jane's father cried: "Twins! Twin teddy-bears - as like as two apples in a bowl!"

(He did not notice the difference in their eyes: that was the kind of thing he would never notice.)

He darted forward, snatched up each teddy-bear by a leg and began juggling with them - throwing them up, one after the other, very quickly, and catching them as quickly, so that there were always two teddy-bears whirling round in the air. He sometimes juggled with apples like this, until Jane's mother told him to stop before he dropped one and bruised it.

Both the little girls were jumping about and shouting to him to stop, as he meant them to. But Lucinda's shouts turned into screams and then into long, screeching sobs. Jane's father stopped at once and thrust both teddy-bears into her arms and tried to hug her and kiss her and talk to her gently, saying over and over again that he hadn't hurt the teddies one bit - they'd liked it - and he was very, very, very sorry. But Lucinda wriggled away from him and threw Jane's teddy away, hard, so that it hit the bedroom wall with a smack; and she went on sobbing.

In the end, Jane's father left them. You could see that he was really upset.

Lucinda stopped crying. She said: "Sorry! He'll be sorry!"

"What do you mean?" asked Jane.

"Didn't you see the look my teddy gave your father out of his magic black eyes?"

"No," said Jane. "My teddy-bear likes my father, even when he throws him up into the air. And my teddy can look at him better than your teddy, because my teddy has *real* teddy eyes. I don't believe your teddy can look at all with woolwork eyes. Not as well as my teddy, anyway."

"Your teddy has silly eyes," said Lucinda. "Yours is a silly teddy. Silly Teddy, Silly Teddy - that's you're teddy's name now."

"No it isn't," said Jane.

"Yes, it is," said Lucinda. "And my teddy is called Black Teddy. And your father will be sorry that he threw Black Teddy up into the air, so that Black Teddy had to look at him with his magic eyes."

Jane wanted to say something back; but her mother came in, rather anxiously, having heard about the juggling. She made the little girls get into their beds at once, and then she tucked them up, and kissed them goodnight, and went out, turning out the light.

They did not speak again. Perhaps Lucinda went quickly to sleep - Jane did not know. Jane herself burrowed under the bedclothes and then whispered in her teddy's ear: "I don't like Black Teddy, do you? But he's not staying long…"

The next morning, after breakfast, Jane's father was washing up when he broke a cup.

"Oh, really!" said his wife.

"It's only one of the cheap ones," he said.

"There isn't such a thing as a cheap cup," she retorted. "If you go on breaking cups, I can't let you wash up."

"I'm planning to break the whole set," said Jane's father.

And no more was said; but Lucinda whispered to Jane, "Black Teddy did that."

"Did what?"

"Made him break that cup. Black Teddy ill-wished him to do it, with a look from his magic eyes."

"I don't believe it."

"Oh, Black Teddy can easily do that. He's ill-wished my father so that he's broken something, and my mother's got angry, and then my father's got angry, and then they've both screamed and screamed at each other, and broken more things; and Black Teddy ill-wished it all with his magic eyes. Just as he ill-wished your father."

Jane wanted to shout: "I don't believe it!" But she was afraid of what Lucinda might say back. She was afraid of Lucinda, or of Black Teddy. So she just turned away.

That Saturday morning Jane's mother took the little girls out with her when she went shopping. Jane said it would be better if they left their teddy-bears at home, each on a separate bed. So they did.

When they got home, Jane went to her room to make sure that her teddy-bear was all right. He sat exactly as she had left him she thought, fully dressed - but then she saw that his balaclava helmet was on back to front. She trembled with anger as she put it right.

Lucinda had come into the room just behind her. "You did that!" said Jane. "You turned his balaclava round so that he couldn't see."

"He can't see, anyway, with those silly eyes," said Lucinda. "And I didn't touch him. Black Teddy just ill-wished it to happen to him and it did."

"It wasn't Black Teddy, it was you," said Jane. "And my teddy can see, except when his balaclava's on back to front."

"Your silly teddy can't see, ever. But Black Teddy, if he wanted to - Black Teddy could see through the back of a balaclava helmet, and through doors, and through walls; he can see through everything when he wants to ill-wish with his magic eyes."

Jane stamped her foot and shouted: "Go away!"

Lucinda said: "I'm going away tomorrow morning and I'm never coming back. You hate me."

Jane said: "Yes, I hate you!"

At that moment, Jane's mother came to call them to dinner, and she overheard what Jane had said. She was very angry with her, and she petted Lucinda, who allowed herself to be petted. Jane saw Lucinda staring at her with her Pontefract eyes from under Jane's mother's chin.

They sat down to dinner; but Jane's father was not in his place. "We've run out of orange squash," said Jane's mother. "He's just gone to the corner shop to get some."

"Is it far?" asked Lucinda.

"Just along our street and across the road," said Jane's mother. "You can start eating, Lucinda."

"Does he have to cross a busy road?" asked Lucinda.

"What?" said Jane's mother. "Oh, yes, busy on a Saturday. But that won't delay him. He's only to wait to cross the road."

Five minutes later, Lucinda asked if she could have a drink of water, as there still wasn't any orange squash. Jane's mother got some from the tap, and looked at the clock. "Where can he have got to?"

"I hope he's all right," said Lucinda.

"What do you mean, child?"

"I hope he's not been run over," said Lucinda, looking at Jane as she spoke.

"What rubbish!" said Jane's mother, and sat down suddenly with her hands clasped tightly in her lap.

At that moment Jane's father walked in with the orange squash. He was surprised that his wife was angry with him for having been so long. He explained that he'd met a friend in the corner shop, and they'd got talking. The friends wanted him to go to a darts match that evening, and he'd said yes.

"Leaving me to babysit?" said Jane's

mother.

Jane's father said he hadn't thought of that; but he offered to take Jane and Lucinda to the playground in the Park that afternoon. So it was agreed.

Again, the teddy-bears were left at home. Just before they set out for the Park, Lucinda said she wanted to wear her bobble-hat after all, and ran back into Jane's room to get it. Jane wondered; but her father was holding her fast by the hand, so she couldn't follow Lucinda.

When they came back from the Park, Jane went straight into her bedroom, and - sure enough - there was her teddy with his balaclava on back to front. She put it right. Lucinda, smiling in the doorway, said: "How naughty of Black Teddy!" Jane glared at her.

That evening, after Jane's father had gone off to his darts match, they watched television. At bedtime, there was Jane's teddy with his balaclava on back to front again; but this time Jane didn't bother to put it right until she was in bed, and her mother was just going to turn out the light. Then she took of the balclava and other clothes, and she took her teddy-bear right down under the bedclothes, and whispered: "Black Teddy is only staying until tomorrow morning. Then he's going home with Lucinda on the coach." She fell asleeep with her teddy-bear in her arms.

She woke because Lucinda was shaking her. Lucinda had drawn back the curtains so that moonlight streamed into the room. She stood by Jane's bed, and in the moonlight her face looked whiter and her eyes blacker than by daylight. She was holding Black Teddy right up to the side of her face.

She said softly to Jane: "Don't make a noise, but listen! Can you hear someone crying?"

"Crying?"

"Sobbing and sobbing. It must be your mother sobbing."

Jane was frightened. "I don't think I can hear her. Why should she be sobbing?"

"Because Black Teddy ill-wished your father with his magic eyes."

"She wouldn't cry because of that," said Jane firmly. And she was certain now that she couldn't hear anything.

"Ah, but she would cry, when she heard what happened to your father on his way home from the darts match, after dark."

"What happened to him?" asked Jane. She hadn't meant to ask; she didn't want to ask; she didn't believe what Lucinda was going to say.

Lucinda turned Black Teddy so that he was facing Jane; she brought him forward so that his black eyes were looking into Jane's eyes. "Listen to what Black Teddy ill-wished," said Lucinda. "You remember that corner of the Park where we took a short cut? You remember that slimy pond that your father said was very deep? You remember that thick bush that grows just beside that pond? You remember?"

"Yes," said Jane faintly.

"Your father decided to take a short cut home in the dark after the darts match. He was crossing that corner of the Park by the pond and the bush. It was very dark; it was very lonely. There was someone hiding behind the bush, waiting for your father."

"Oh, no!"

"He jumped out at your father from behind and hit him on the head, hard and then he dragged him towards the pond -"

"No, no, no!" With what seemed one movement Jane was out of bed and into the sitting room and there was her mother dozing in front of the television set. She woke up when Jane rushed in, and Jane rushed into her arms. What Jane said was such a muddle and so frantic that her mother thought she had been having nightmares. While she was trying to calm her, Jane's father walked in, very pleased with his darts evening, and perfectly safe and sound.

They tried to understand what Jane tried to tell them. They looked into Jane's bedroom, but there was Lucinda in bed, apparently sound asleep, with Black Teddy clasped in her arms. Even the curtains were drawn close.

They were cross with Jane when she said she wasn't going to sleep in the same room as Lucinda's Black Teddy, but in the end they gave way. They wrapped her in rugs and she slept on the couch in the sitting room, and Lucinda and Black Teddy had Jane's room to themselves.

"And I don't want to play with her tomorrow morning, and I don't want to see her off at the coach-station, or be with her and her Black Teddy at all!" said Jane, when they said a last goodnight to her.

On Sunday morning they all had breakfast together, but the little girls spoke not a word to each other. After breakfast Jane's mother said that she would help Lucinda get ready to go home, and Jane's father said he would take Jane to the playground while she was doing that. In the playground, Jane's father often looked at his watch; and they didn't stay there very long. When they got back, Jane's mother and Lucinda had gone. Probably only just gone: Jane's father had timed their return very carefully.

He said: "Well, that's that! Poor little girl!" Jane said: "She was horrible, and she had a horrible Black Teddy."

"She's very unhappy at home," said her father. "We must make allowances. Her mother and father fight like cat and dog. She suffers. That's why your mother asked her for a weekend; but it didn't work."

"Oh," said Jane, but she didn't feel sorry for Lucinda at all. She went off to her bedroom - her own bedroom that she wouldn't have to share with Lucinda and Black Teddy any more. And there sat her own dear teddy-bear on her bed, waiting for her. He had his balaclava helmet on back to front, as Lucinda must have arranged it before she left; but that was for the very last time. No more of Black Teddy and his ill-wishing, ever again...

She gazed happily at her teddy-bear; but as she gazed, her happiness seemed to falter, to die in her. She gazed, and thought that her teddy-bear seemed somehow not his usual self. There was something odd about the way he sat; something odd about his paws; something odd about his ears -

She snatched him up and pulled off the balaclava helmet: a pair of black woollen eyes stared at her.

She rushed back to her father, crying: "She's taken the wrong teddy! Lucinda's stolen my teddy-bear!" She gabbled and wept together.

Her father acted instantly. "Come on!" he said. "Bring him with you, and we're off. They've got ten minutes start on us to the coach-station, but we might be in time. We must catch them before the coach leaves with Lucinda and Lucinda's suitcase with your teddy in it. Come on - run!"

They tore out of the house, Jane's father gripping Jane's hand, and Jane gripping Black Teddy. They ran and ran: they had to wait at the main road for a gap in the traffic, and then across, and past the corner shop, and by the short cut across the Park - there was that dreadful bush beside that dreadful pond, only it was all bright and busy this Sunday morning - and on, down another street, and then another, and Jane was quite breathless, and there was the coach-station! They went rushing in, and Jane's father seemed to know where Lucinda's coach would be, and there it was! There it was, with Jane's mother talking to the driver, no doubt about putting Lucinda off at the right place, where she would be met. And there was Lucinda herself, already sitting in the coach, with her suitcase in the rack above her head.

"Stay there!" said her father to Jane, and he took Black Teddy from her and climbed into the coach. He hadn't time to say anything to Jane's mother, who stared in amazement; so Jane explained to her mother - and to the coach-driver - while she watched what her father was doing.

Once he was in the coach, Jane's father stopped being in a hurry and being excited. He walked to the empty seat next to Lucinda and sat down in it and spoke to her, showing her Black Teddy. (Jane could see all this very clearly through the window of the coach.) He talked to her, and while he talked he took the trousers and jersey off Black Teddy and stuffed them into his pocket. Then he put Black Teddy into Lucinda's arms, but she just let him fall into her lap. Jane's father went on talking, and still he didn't take the suitcase from the rack and snatch Jane's teddy from it, as Jane expected every minute.

At last Jane's father took a handkerchief from his pocket and began dabbing Lucinda's cheeks with it. So Lucinda was crying.

And at last Lucinda stood up in her seat and reached for her suitcase in the rack and brought it down and opened it and took Jane's teddy from it and gave it to Jane's father. Then he put the suitcase back for her, and tried to put his arm round her and kiss her goodbye, but she wouldn't let him. Then he got off the coach with Jane's teddy-bear.

Jane's father thanked the coach-driver for delaying those few minutes, and he handed Jane her teddy-bear, and she hugged him.

Then the coach was off. It moved out of the station towards the great London Road. They were all waving goodbye to Lucinda, even Jane; but she never waved, never looked back.

The coach stopped at the lights before the great London Road. They couldn't see Lucinda any more, because of the sun's dazzling on the glass of her window. But they could see the window beginning to crawl down: Lucinda must be winding it down from the inside. And Black Teddy appeared at the gap at the top of the window.

The lights changed and the coach moved on again, into the traffic on the great London

Road, gathered speed with the rest of the traffic...

And Black Teddy fell from the window - no, he was *thrown* from the window. Thrown into the middle of the rushing, crushing, cruel traffic.

That was his end.

And the coach went on, out of sight.

Of the three watchers, no one moved; no one spoke. Jane hugged and hugged her own dear teddy to her, and the yellow fur on the top of his head began to be wet with tears. Against her will, she was weeping for what had happened - for all that had happened. She wept for Black Teddy. She wept for Lucinda, too. Now, at last, she felt sorry for Lucinda; and the sorrow was like a pain inside her.

KBW

BY FARRUKH DHONDY

Tahir's gone now. No one to play chess with. I ask my dad for a game and he says he has a union meeting to attend this evening. "Young Habib would've given you three in a row with one hand tied behind his blooming back," he says as he goes out.

My dad says they're going to move an Irish family in. He knows that I shall miss Tahir. "Maybe young Paddy will know some chess," he says.

Their flat was exactly like ours, except the other way round, like when you see a thing in a mirror. Like twins growing out of each other our two flats were. And I was Tahir's best friend. The windows are still smashed, but the flat's been boarded up, like some others on our estate. It goes for kilometres. You must've heard of it, it's called the Devonmount estate, Borough of Hackney. I shan't go to cricket practice today. I dropped out after Tahir left. We joined the team together so I think it's only right that we pull out together.

My mother doesn't understand. She says, "Go on out and do something. Go and play cricket, you can't help the way the world is. Don't sit there looking like a month of wet Sundays."

Dad understands. "Son, you're right. Don't have no truck with racialist swine." He always talks like that. Mum still needles him about being a Communist and he always replies that he's a Red in her bed, and the day she tries to put him under for his political views, he'll leave. They all know my dad on the estate. Twenty-two years he's been here.

I was born here and went to school here, to Devonmount Juniors and then Devonmount Comprehensive, no less. Tahir came here eight months ago. His dad came from

Bangladesh, because they were driven out by the riots. That's what Tahir told me. He came straight into the fourth form. I took him to school the first day. My dad introduced himself to Mr Habib as soon as they moved in, and he said to me at dinner that day, "My boy, a Bengali family has moved in next door, and I've told mister that you are going to take master to school. He's in your form and I want you to take him in and stick him outside the headmaster's office."

That's how I met Tahir. I asked him what games he liked and he said cricket so I took him to Mr Hadley, the local vicar who runs the cricket team, and Tahir bowled for us. He was great. He lit up when they said they wanted to try him. Mr Hadley gave him the bat and bowled to him, and Tahir struck it hard to mid-off and was caught first go. Then Hadley gave him the ball. Tahir stroked it like it was a pigeon or something and when he looked up there was a shine in his eyes, same as you get out of the toe of a shoe when you put spit on the leather. He took a short run and bowled that ball. It spun at an amazing speed to leg-side.

"What do we have here?" Mr Hadley said, and his glasses gleamed. Tahir was our best spin bowler. He took four wickets in the match against the Mercer's Estate. When we won that match we were sure to get to the finals with the Atlanta Atlases. They were the best estate club going. If we beat them we'd be champs of Hackney. If you don't live in Hackney and don't live on the Devonmount, you don't know what that means. But I'll tell you what it means. It means Vietnam, North Vietnam that is, beating America in a war. That's what it means, a little country with a lot of determination, and without two ha'pennies to rub together, beating what my dad calls the biggest military machine ever built by man or money. Because ours is the worst estate. The flats are filthy and the stairs and the courtyard are never cleaned. There's coal dumps in the yards and half the places are boarded up. You should have seen the Habib's flat. Water pouring down the wall of one bedroom, the wallpaper peeling off like scabs, and the roof-plaster all torn to bits. My dad said that it was nothing less than a crying shame for a workers' government to treat the workers so. My mum said she remembered when she was a little girl, and they ought to be thankful for a bathful of water which was hot.

The door of their flat has been forced open and the young ones play in there. That's what they call kids who still go to primary school on the Devonmount. I'm not a little'un any more, I'm twelve and I'm not interested in climbing the garbage carts and pulling bits off people's cars and playing cowboys and indians or hide and seek or cops and robbers in the empty flats. I used to be, and in those days I couldn't see why everyone on the estate complained about it. To me the empty flats were space. They gave you the feeling not that you belonged there, but that the place belonged to you so you could never leave it. Last year they built an adventure playground for the little 'uns on an empty sight, and they went in hordes there, but after a while they didn't like it, they stopped going and started back in the empty flats again. There was nothing to nick in the adventure playground but the empties. You can find and flog all-sorts of things around here. There are some blokes on the estate who'll give you quite a few pence for a load of pipes or even for boards and doorknobs and toilet seats and that, and the kids on the estate break in and rip everything up. It's only when a flat has been completely ripped up that it becomes a place to play in. It gets cleaned out like a corpse gutted by sharks. I walked through their flat yesterday and it's been done over.

When Tahir's family first moved in, the people around didn't like it. They didn't go to the trouble of worrying them, but the boys from C Block came to our building and painted "Niggers Out" on the landing. My dad said it was a shame and he gave me some turps and a rag and asked me to clean it off, but I couldn't, it wouldn't come off. He said it was an insult to coloureds, and I know it was because the lads from C Block don't like coloured people - they're always picking on Pakis and coons when they're in a gang. My mum says they only do it because they're really scared of them, but I don't think they are. When Tahir and I came home from school together they used to shout, "Want to buy an elephant?" and all that bollocks. Tahir never took any notice. He always walked looking straight ahead, but even though he didn't understand what they were saying, he'd become very silent and not say a word to me all the rest of the way. I still think I was his best friend. There was always six of them and they were bigger than us. Sometimes they'd even come to our block and shout from downstairs. If Tahir's father heard them he'd come out on to the gallery and shout back at them. I think he was a very brave man. He wasn't scared of anyone and he'd say, "Get out, swine," because those were the only swear words in English that he knew. He didn't speak English very much and when my dad met him on the stairs or invited him round for a cup of tea, he'd just say, "It's very kind, don't trouble, please don't trouble." Tahir told me once that his father was a karate expert and could break three bricks with one hand. And he was strong. One day when I was in their flat, he lifted a whole big refrigerator all by himself from the bottom of the stairs.

The trouble all started with the newspapers. There was a story in the *Sun* one day which said that two people in London had died of typhoid. My mum and dad talked about it at home and Mrs Biggles, my mum's mate, said that a girl in C Block had been taken to St Margaret's Hospital and was under observation there. The girl was called Jenny and we knew her 'cause she used to go to the same school as my little sister Lynn.

The story went around the estate that there was typhus in the East End, and everybody

183

was talking about it. Then a funny thing happened. We play cricket down in Haggerston Park and after the game, when Mr Hadley has locked the kit away in the hut at the corner, he takes us all to the vicarage and he gives us bags of crisps and cups of cocoa, and lets us listen to his records. Well, this last Saturday, we had a lot of kids turn up for cricket practice. Usually there's only the team, about thirteen lads, but this time there was eighteen because Mr Hadley said we had to have proper trials for the juniors team. We all sat around while James and Mr Hadley made the cocoa. He peeped around the door and said, "There's only seven mugs, so you'll have to share the cocoa."

We said, "Right ho, umpire," because that's what he liked to be called. Sometimes he tells us, if he's feeling like talking about church, that vicars are umpires from God and that life is like a test match between good and evil. I think Mr Hadley explains things well, but I still don't believe in it. My dad says that Hadley should stick to cricket and not brainwash the team, because my dad's dead against the Christians. He's an aetheist but our mum tells us not to take any notice of him, because she believes in God.

Anyway, on this Saturday, James brought in the cups of cocoa to the team and gave them to every second person, as two people had to share. We were sitting in a circle on the carpet and Nick was changing the records. Every now and then someone would get up and there'd be an argument about whether to have David Essex or Slade on next. Tahir never said a word. He was holding a steaming cup of cocoa and you could see the gaps in his teeth when he smiled. The lads would ask him to whistle and he'd always try but he couldn't do it on account of the big gap in his front teeth.

Next to Tahir there was a boy called Alan, and when Tahir had taken a few sips of the cocoa after it had cooled, he passed it on to him. The rest of us were fighting for the mugs, just mucking about sort of, and eating crisps at the same time. I was watching this boy Alan, who had freckles and a thin face which looked scared most of the time, and I could see that he didn't want to take the cup from Tahir.

"Have it, I've finished," Tahir said.

Alan said he didn't want any cocoa, so Tahir turned to try and give the mug back to James.

"Everyone's got one," James said. "They're sharing if they haven't."

"You didn't get," Tahir said, smiling upward at James.

"I'll share someone's," James replied, but when Tahir tried to give him his cup, he said, "No, that's all right, you have the rest, I'll get some later."

Tahir put his cup down in the middle of the carpet. All the cocoa from the other mugs was finished, but no one wanted to pick up Tahir's mug. Then it struck me. Mr Hadley shouted from the kitchen that the milk was finished, and there was a sort of silence in the room.

Tahir was searching the other faces.

"Anybody could drink it," he said.

Nobody picked up the mug. It stood on the carpet, not even half drunk. I looked at the others. A second before they'd been laughing and talking, but now there was only the sound of the record player. I think Tahir understood. I looked at Alan. He had a look on his face like a dog that's been whipped. The others were looking at him too.

"I don't want any," he said.

Mr Hadley, his red face still shining with the sweat of the game, came in and said that it had been a damned hard selection and if we put in a bit of practice we could beat the Atlases. "Fine cricket," he said, and he rubbed his hands as usual. "With fine weather it'll be finer."

Tahir was silent on the way home. He kept looking at his feet as we walked, and he looked thinner and even smaller than he normally looked.

When I got home, Mrs Biggles was in the kitchen. "They suspect typhus, the girl's shaking with fever and the poor dear didn't even recognize her own mother," she was saying. She was asking Lynn questions about the girl Jenny who was in hospital "It's not known here," the doctor had said to her mother, "It's the foreigners have brought it in, that's for sure, from Istanbul and Pakistan and now from that Ugandan Asian's place. We've never had these things here," he went on.

"It's the blacks bring these things in here..." she said.

My mum went dead silent. After Mrs Biggles had left, my dad put his mug of tea on the table and said he didn't want Mrs Biggles and her filthy mouth in his house, but Mum pretended she didn't hear and kept looking at the telly screen.

Another odd thing happened, on the

following Monday. I woke up and dressed for school. Usually by the time my cornflakes are on the table, Dad's gone to work, but I found him in the kitchen that morning. He looked worried. He was sitting at the kitchen table with his hair brushed back and shiny with hair oil. He was talking to Mum, and then he took his coat and left. Mum said the people on the estate were rats and they needed poisoning, or leastways they deserved it. "He took him to the pub once," she said, "just once as far as I know."

"Who?" I asked.

"That Mr Habib from next door, your Tahir's father, even though the poor man couldn't drink on account of his religion, he had to drag him along just to show everyone."

"Who took him?"

"Them people from C," she said, "they've painted things on our door. I wish Dad would call the police."

As I walked out to school I turned to the door and it said 'KBW' in big black letters.

Dad was furious with Mum for telling me about it, and they had a right row that evening. Mum had scrubbed it off the door with sandpaper.

"Did you come back with Tahir?" she asked.

Tahir had been at school that day, but he behaved a bit strange. He wasn't there for the last lesson and I reckoned he must have hopped it.

"What does it mean?" I asked my dad, remembering the letters.

"It means your dad is poking his nose into other people's business," my mum said.

"You know what they painted on our door, son?" my dad asked.

"I saw it," I said.

"It means Keep Britain White," Dad said. He looked grey in the face and serious. You know what that means, son. It used to be the Jews in the thirties, now it's bleedin' Indians and Pakistanis. Some people have seen you with Tahir."

"More like they've seen you chatting like old friends to Habash, or whatever his name is," Mum said.

"I've seen a lot of it and I hoped you wouldn't grow up in a world with these anti-working-class prejudices. I don't care what your mum says, but we've got to fight it. I've been fighting it, and I hope my son and grandson will fight it too."

190

"And a lot of good it's done you," Mum said.

But I was kind of proud of my dad.

"They are fascist scum, lad," he said. He always calls me 'lad' when he gets to lecturing about his politics.

"Don't go putting your ideas into the boy's head, you leave him to think as he pleases."

Dad ignored her. He sat with his palms on his knees and with his tall back pushed against the chair, the way he always did when he thought he was teaching me the facts of life.

"You know this typhoid, lad," he said. "People are blaming the Habibs for bringing it in. But any law court in this country knows they're innocent. It's ignorance and superstition. This girl Jenny went to Spain on the school trip with our Lynn, didn't she?" This was said more to Mum than to me.

I hardly slept at all that night. The next day the papers said that the girl Jenny was worse and that several cases of typhoid had been found and more people had been put under observation in the East End hospitals. I was thinking that I knew why the cricket team hadn't wanted to touch Tahir's cocoa. I was wishing I had picked it up. I knew that Tahir must be thinking the same thing too. It struck me that he must have thought that I had the same idea as the rest of them.

Sometimes I have funny dreams and that's when I can't sleep. That night I dreamt of the letters K B W painted up across our door, and then the letters spread out with other letters on to the whole of the estate, and the letters growing and becoming bigger and bigger till they were too heavy and had to come crashing down, falling on top of me, the K like two great legs and the W spinning round like giant compasses.

I went very tired to school. I didn't tell Mum about the dream. Tahir wasn't in the playground and he wasn't at registration. I thought he might be late, but he never came late, and then it struck me that I knew he wouldn't come to school that day.

I stayed in that night and so did Dad. He usually goes down to the pub for a jar, but he didn't bother that night. He turned on the telly and I could see from the way he folded his legs, and from his eyes which were glued on the screen but not taking in the programme, that he was worried. He usually starts on at Lynn when he's like that, asks her to polish her shoes for school the next day and for her homework and everything. It felt to me too as though something was about to happen and it did.

I heard the crash and then another thud and another crash of glass and a woman screaming. It was Tahir's mother. Dad sprang up from his chair. I felt that he had been expecting it. He rushed to the door. Mum came out of the kitchen. The crash of brick or stone sounded as though it was in our own house. Dad opened the door and went out on to the gallery.

"Bastards, cowards!" I heard. It was Mr Habib shouting his lungs out.

Dad rushed back into the flat. "There's twenty of them out there."

"Shall I call the police?" Mum asked.

Dad didn't answer. Everyone hates coppers on our estate, and no one ever calls them. Coppers don't need invitations. I could hear the blokes downstairs shouting. Mum pushed Lynn away from her and went out on to the gallery.

Mr Habib was still shouting, "You are all bastards, white bastards."

Then we heard the running steps on the stairs. The blokes were coming up, and they were shouting too: "Paki filth," and, "The girl's dead."

It was all hell. Mr Habib went in and got Tahir's cricket bat. The blokes from C Block had bottles. There was more crashing of glass and Mrs Habib kept screaming things in Indian and I could hear Tahir crying and shouting and a lot of thumping.

"Why don't you help him?" my mum shouted to Dad. "What kind of bloody Communist are you?" But Dad was pushing her into the kitchen."

"Shut your mouth," he said to her. He never talks like that normally, but he looked as though he'd pissed himself. "Let the police handle this. There's twenty of them out there."

By the time the police came, with sirens blaring, pulling into the courtyard, jumping out and slamming their car doors, the blokes were gone.

I said, "Mum, I'm going out," and before she could stop me I went to the door and unbolted it. Other people had come out of their flats. The galleries of all floors were now full of people trying to see what had happened. The police called an ambulance, and they took Mr Habib, who was lying outside his door groaning, to hospital. Tahir was bending over him when the coppers came with an Indian bloke and started asking questions. Tahir looked up at me as I stepped out, and he looked away. His dad had all blood streaming down his face. The day after, the blood marks were still there, all over the gallery.

Two hours later, we were all still awake. It was still as death outside and silent.

"I'll take it up with the council," my dad said. I knew what he felt. He had wanted to help Tahir's dad, I am sure, but he felt helpless. There were too many of the others, he couldn't have said nothing.

"I wouldn't be seen dead at that girl's funeral," Dad said after a while.

Four Indian blokes came and took Tahir and his mum and all their stuff away that same night and we could hear the coppers who'd stayed behind arguing with them.

The next day at cricket Mr Hadley asked me where Tahir was. The other boys told him the whole story, that bricks had been thrown through their windows and that Tahir's dad was in hospital.

Mr Hadley knew our school and he turned up there the next day. The headmaster sent for Tahir and for me from class and we walked together to the office without a word. Mr

Hadley was there. He said he was sorry to hear that Tahir's family had been in an unfortunate incident and that he wanted Tahir to come to cricket practice.

Tahir answered all his questions about where they were living and that. He said, "Yes, sir," when Mr Hadley said that he must realize that he had a lot of good friends like me and that wherever he lived he must continue to play for Devonmount. He said, "Yes, sir," his legs apart, his hands folded behind his back, his head bent and his lips tight together, his eyes moving from Mr Hadley's face to the floor. But he never came again.

MART WAS MY BEST FRIEND

BY MICHAEL ROSEN

Mart was my best friend.
I thought he was great,
but one day he tried to do for me.

I had a hat - a woolly one
and I loved that hat.
It was warm and tight.
My mum had knitted it
and I wore it everywhere.

One day me and Mart were out
and we were standing at a bus-stop
and suddenly
he goes and grabs my hat
and chucked it over the wall.
He thought I was going to go in there
and get it out.
He thought he'd make me do that
because he knew I liked that hat so much
I wouldn't be able to stand being without it.

197

He was right -
I could hardly bear it.
I was really scared I'd never get it back.
But I never let on.
I never showed it on my face.
I just waited.
"Aren't you going to get your hat?"
he says.
"Your hat's gone," he says.
"Your hat's over the wall."
I looked the other way.

But I could still feel on my head
how he had pulled it off.
"Your hat's over the wall," he says.
I didn't say a thing.

Then the bus came round the corner
 at the end of the road.

If I go home without my hat
I'm going to walk through the door
and mum's going to say,
"Where's your hat?"
and if I say,
"It's over the wall,"
she's going to say,

"What's it doing there?"
and I'm going to say,
"Mart chucked it over,"
and she's going to say,
"Why didn't you go for it?"
and what am I going to say then?
What am I going to say then?

The bus was coming up.
"Aren't you going over for your hat?
There won't be another bus for ages,"
Mart says.

The bus was coming closer.
"You've lost your hat now,"
Mart says.
The bus stopped.
I got on
Marg got on
The bus moved off.

"You've lost your hat," Mart says.

"You've lost your hat," Mart says.

Two stops ahead, was ours.
"Are you going indoors without it?" Mart
says.

I didn't say a thing.
The bus stopped.

Mart got up,
and dashed downstairs.
He'd got off one stop early.
I got off when we got to our stop.

I went home
walked through the door
"Where's your hat?" Mum says.
"Over a wall," I said.
"What's it doing there?" she says.
"Mart chucked it over there," I said.
"But you haven't left it there, have you?"
she says.
"Yes," I said.
"Well don't you ever come asking me to
make you anything like that again.
You make me tired, you do."

Later,
I was drinking some orange juice.
The front door-bell rang.
It was Mart.
He had the hat in his hand.

He handed it to me - and went.
I shut the front door -
put on the hat
and walked into the kitchen.
Mum looked up.
"You don't need to wear your hat indoors
do you?" she said.
"I will for a bit," I said.
And I did.

ACKNOWLEDGEMENTS

The editors and publishers would like to thank the following
authors, agents and publishers for permission to reprint
the following material:

How Anthony Made a Friend by Jan Mark from *Nothing to be
Afraid Of*, Kestrel Books, reproduced by kind permission of Penguin
Books
Lenny's Red Letter Day from *I'm Trying to Tell You* by Bernard
Ashley, Kestrel Books © Bernard Ashley 1981, reproduced by kind
permission of Penguin Books Ltd.
The Great Leapfrog Contest from *Best Stories of William Saroyan*,
Faber & Faber Ltd, reprinted by permission of Laurence Pollinger
Ltd and the William Saroyan Foundation.
The Mile from *The Fib and Other Stories* by George Layton,
Longman, © George Layton 1978
Duffings by E. W. Hildick, from *In a Few Words* edited by Bradley,
Edward Arnold Ltd.
Cleo the Vigilant from *Here Tomorrow Gone Today* by Tim
Kennemore, reprinted by permission of Faber & Faber Ltd.
The Hitch-Hiker from *The Wonderful World of Henry Sugar* by
Roald Dahl, Jonathan Cape Ltd.
After You, My Dear Alphonse from *The Lottery and Other Stories* by
Shirley Jackson, © Shirley Jackson 1943, 1949, Farrar, Strauss and
Giroux Inc., reprinted by permission of Brandt and Brandt Literary
Agents Inc
Thingy by Chris Powling from *Daredevils and Scaredycats*, Blackie
& Son Ltd.
KBW by Farrukh Dhondy, from *East End at Your Feet*, Macmillan.
Black Eyes by Philippa Pearce from *Black Eyes and other
Spinechillers*, edited by Galway, Pepper Press, 1981

Every effort has been made by the publishers to trace the copyright
owners. In the event of an erroneous credit, or no credit, copyright
owners should contact the publishers who will correct on subsequent
reprints.

Illustrations by Annabel Large and Linda Birch

ANGEL FACE
Narinder Dhami

Catherine's life is in a mess. She has no friends, and she's the most unfanciable girl in the class. Aidan's cool, good looking and girl-crazy – and girls are crazy about him. He's just about perfect – except that he's dead! When Aidan gets the chance to revisit Earth as Catherine's guardian angel, he can't wait – until he sees her! But the tables are turned when Aidan's plan to sort out Catherine's life begin to go seriously wrong. Will God recall Aidan to Cloud Nine – or will there be a miracle before time runs out for both of them?

A hilarious, heavenly tale about growing up.

Collins
An *Imprint* of HarperCollins*Publishers*

STREET CHILD
Berlie Doherty

Jim Jarvis is a runaway. When his mother dies, Jim is all alone in the workhouse and is desperate to escape. But London in the 1860s is a dangerous and lonely place for a small boy and life is a constant battle for survival. Just when Jim finds some friends, he is snatched away and made to work for the remorselessly cruel Grimy Nick, constantly guarded by his vicious dog, Snipe.

Jim's gripping adventure is based on the true story of the orphan whose plight inspired Doctor Barnardo to set up his famous children's refuge.

Collins
An *Imprint* of HarperCollins*Publishers*

SWEET 'N' SOUR
Nina Milton

Low Hee's been living happily with his grandmother in Malaysia since he was born, so he's pretty annoyed when his father returns after seven years to take him to live in England. Life above the take-away restaurant is bleak – he can't speak any English or understand school *and* he's got a little sister no one has told him about.

But Low's life changes dramatically when he has an accident and changes places with Liang, the mysterious boy he has seen from his window. He is swept up into a dream-like adventure of slavery and danger where there seems to be no escape.

Collins
An *Imprint of HarperCollinsPublishers*

A RUBY, A RUG AND A PRINCE CALLED DOUG
Kaye Umansky

Doug is just an ordinary sort of prince, until he's sent to St Charming's and forced to wear silly clothes. Ruby looks like Little Red Riding Hood, but no wolf would ever mess with her. Ray is a bodyguard of little brain. When travelling through the deep forest something terrible happens! Ambushed by a dastardly dandy, Doug loses his dirty old rug, Ruby loses her money and Ray loses his nerve. Together they must find the rug - and save the kingdom.

A wild and crazy adventure.

Collins
An *Imprint of* HarperCollins*Publishers*

Order Form

To order direct from the publishers, just make a list of the titles you want and fill in the form below:

Name ....

Address ....

....

....

Send to: Dept 6, HarperCollins Publishers Ltd, Westerhill Road, Bishopbriggs, Glasgow G64 2QT.

Please enclose a cheque or postal order to the value of the cover price, plus:

UK & BFPO: Add £1.00 for the first book, and 25p per copy for each addition book ordered.

Overseas and Eire: Add £2.95 service charge. Books will be sent by surface mail but quotes for airmail despatch will be given on request.

A 24-hour telephone ordering service is avail-able to Visa and Access card holders: 041-772 2281